Contents

Secret Key #1 – Guessing Is Not Guesswork.

You probably know that guessing is a good idea on the MCAS- unlike other standardized tests, there is no penalty for getting a wrong answer. Even if you have no idea about a question, you still have a 20-25% chance of getting it right.

Most test takers do not understand the impact that proper guessing can have on their score. Unless you score extremely high, guessing will significantly contribute to your final score.

Monkeys Take the MCAS

What most test takers don't realize is that to insure that 20-25% chance, you have to guess randomly. If you put 20 monkeys in a room to take the MCAS, assuming they answered once per question and behaved themselves, on average they would get 20-25% of the questions correct. Put 20 test takers in the room, and the average will be much lower among guessed questions. Why?

1. MCAS intentionally writes deceptive answer choices that "look" right. A test taker has no idea about a question, so picks the "best looking" answer, which is often wrong. The monkey has no idea what looks good and what doesn't, so will consistently be lucky about 20-25% of the time.
2. Test takers will eliminate answer choices from the guessing pool based on a hunch or intuition. Simple but correct answers often get excluded, leaving a 0% chance of being correct. The monkey has no clue, and often gets lucky with the best choice.

This is why the process of elimination endorsed by most test courses is flawed and detrimental to your performance- test takers don't guess, they make an ignorant stab in the dark that is usually worse than random.

Success Strategy #1

Let me introduce one of the most valuable ideas of this course- the $5 challenge:

You only mark your "best guess" if you are willing to bet $5 on it.
You only eliminate choices from guessing if you are willing to bet $5 on it.

Why $5? Five dollars is an amount of money that is small yet not insignificant, and can really add up fast (20 questions could cost you $100). Likewise, each answer choice on one question of the MCAS will have a small impact on your overall score, but it can really add up to a lot of points in the end.

The process of elimination IS valuable. The following shows your chance of guessing it right:

If you eliminate this many choices:	0	1	2	3
Chance of getting it correct	25%	33%	50%	100%

However, if you accidentally eliminate the right answer or go on a hunch for an incorrect answer, your chances drop dramatically: to 0%. By guessing among all the answer choices, you are GUARANTEED to have a shot at the right answer.

That's why the $5 test is so valuable- if you give up the advantage and safety of a pure guess, it had better be worth the risk.

What we still haven't covered is how to be sure that whatever guess you make is truly random. Here's the easiest way:

Always pick the first answer choice among those remaining.

Such a technique means that you have decided, **before you see a single test question**, exactly how you are going to guess- and since the order of choices tells you nothing about which one is correct, this guessing technique is perfectly random.

Let's try an example-

A test taker encounters the following problem on the mathematics test:

What is the cosine of an angle in a right triangle that is 3 meters on the adjacent side, 5 meters on the hypotenuse, and 4 meters on the opposite side?

A. 1
B. 0.6
C. 0.8
D. 1.25

The test taker has a small idea about this question- he is pretty sure that cosine is opposite over hypotenuse, but he wouldn't bet $5 on it. He knows that cosine is "something" over hypotenuse, and since the hypotenuse is the largest number, he is willing to bet $5 on both choices A and D not being correct. So he is down to B and C. At this point, he guesses B, since B is the first choice remaining.

The test taker is correct by choosing B, since cosine is adjacent over hypotenuse. He only eliminated those choices he was willing to bet money on, AND he did not let his stale memories (often things not known definitely will get mixed up in the exact opposite arrangement in one's head) about the formula for cosine influence his guess. He blindly chose the first remaining choice, and was rewarded with the fruits of a random guess.

This section is not meant to scare you away from making educated guesses or eliminating choices- you just need to define when a choice is worth eliminating. The $5 test, along with a pre-defined random guessing strategy, is the best way to make sure you reap all of the benefits of guessing.

Specific Guessing Techniques

Slang

Scientific sounding answers are better than slang ones. In the answer choices below, choice B is much less scientific and is incorrect, while choice A is a scientific analytical choice and is correct.

Example:

A.) To compare the outcomes of the two different kinds of treatment.

B.) Because some subjects insisted on getting one or the other of the treatments.

Extreme Statements

Avoid wild answers that throw out highly controversial ideas that are proclaimed as established fact. Choice A is a radical idea and is incorrect. Choice B is a calm rational statement. Notice that Choice B does not make a definitive, uncompromising stance, using a hedge word "if" to provide wiggle room.

Example:

A.) Bypass surgery should be discontinued completely.

B.) Medication should be used instead of surgery for patients who have not had a heart attack if they suffer from mild chest pain and mild coronary artery blockage.

Similar Answer Choices

When you have two answer choices that are direct opposites, one of them is usually the correct answer.

Example:

A.) Paragraph 1 described the author's reasoning about the influence of his childhood on his adult life.

B.) Paragraph 2 described the author's reasoning about the influence of his childhood on his adult life.

These two answer choices are very similar and fall into the same family of answer choices. A family of answer choices is when two or three answer choices are very similar. Often two will be opposites and one may show an equality.

Example:

A.) Operation I or Operation II can be conducted at equal cost

B.) Operation I would be less expensive than Operation II

C.) Operation II would be less expensive than Operation I

D.) Neither Operation I nor Operation II would be effective at preventing the spread of cancer.

Note how the first three choices are all related. They all ask about a cost comparison. Beware of immediately recognizing choices B and C as opposites and choosing one of those two. Choice A is in the same family of questions and should be considered as well. However, choice D is not in the same family of questions. It has nothing to do with cost and can be discounted in most cases.

Hedging

When asked for a conclusion that may be drawn, look for critical "hedge" phrases, such as likely, may, can, will often, sometimes, etc, often, almost, mostly, usually, generally, rarely, sometimes. Question writers insert these hedge phrases to cover every possibility. Often an answer will be wrong simply because it leaves no room for exception. Avoid answer choices that have definitive words like "exactly," and "always".

Summary of Guessing Techniques

1. Eliminate as many choices as you can by using the $5 test. Use the common guessing strategies to help in the elimination process, but only eliminate choices that pass the $5 test.
2. Among the remaining choices, only pick your "best guess" if it passes the $5 test.
3. Otherwise, guess randomly by picking the first remaining choice.

Secret Key #2 – Practice Smarter, Not Harder

Many test takers delay the test preparation process because they dread the awful amounts of practice time they think necessary to succeed on the test. We have refined an effective method that will take you only a fraction of the time.

There are a number of "obstacles" in your way on the MCAS. Among these are answering questions, finishing in time, and mastering test-taking strategies. All must be executed on the day of the test at peak performance, or your score will suffer. The MCAS is a mental marathon that has a large impact on your future.

Just like a marathon runner, it is important to work your way up to the full challenge. So first you just worry about questions, and then time, and finally strategy:

Success Strategy #2

1. Find a good source for MCAS practice tests. The sample questions listed at end of this guide would be a good start.
2. If you are willing to make a larger time investment, consider using more than one study guide- often the different approaches of multiple authors will help you "get" difficult concepts.
3. Take a practice test with no time constraints, with all study helps "open book." Take your time with questions and focus on applying the strategies.
4. Take another test, this time with time constraints, with all study helps "open book."
5. Take a final practice test with no open material and time limits. This will be the real test of if you know the material.

If you have time to take more practice tests, just repeat step 5. By gradually exposing yourself to the full rigors of the test environment, you will condition your mind to the stress of test day and maximize your success.

Secret Key #3 – Prepare, Don't Procrastinate

Let me state an obvious fact: if you take the MCAS three times, you will get three different scores. This is due to the way you feel on test day, the level of preparedness you have, and, despite MCAS's claims to the contrary, some tests WILL be easier for you than others.

Since so much depends on your score, you should maximize your chances of success. In order to maximize the likelihood of success, you've got to prepare in advance. This means taking practice tests and spending time learning the information and test taking strategies you will need to succeed.

You can always retake the test more than once, but when you go to take the MCAS, be prepared, be focused, and do your best the first time!

Secret Key #4 – Test Yourself

Everyone knows that time is money. There is no need to spend too much of your time or too little of your time preparing for the MCAS. You should only spend as much of your precious time preparing as is necessary for you to pass it.

Success Strategy #4

Once you have taken a practice test under real conditions of time constraints, then you will know if you are ready for the test or not.

If you have scored extremely high the first time that you take the practice test, then there is not much point in spending countless hours studying. You are already there.

If you are close to a passing score, whether above or below, then you should spend a moderate amount of time studying. Benchmark your abilities by retaking practice tests and seeing how much you have improved. Once you score high enough to have a comfortable margin between your score and a passing, then you are ready.

If you have scored well below where you need, then knuckle down and begin studying in earnest. Check your improvement regularly through the use of practice tests under real conditions. Above all, don't worry, panic, or give up. The key is perseverance!

Then, when you go to take the MCAS, be prepared, be focused, and do your best. Remain confident and remember how well you did on the practice tests. If you can score a passing score on a practice test, then you can do the same on the real thing.

Top 20 Test Taking Tips

1. Carefully follow all the test registration procedures
2. Know the test directions, duration, topics, question types, how many questions
3. Setup a flexible study schedule at least 3-4 weeks before test day
4. Study during the time of day you are most alert, relaxed, and stress free
5. Maximize your learning style; visual learner use visual study aids, auditory learner use auditory study aids
6. Focus on your weakest knowledge base
7. Find a study partner to review with and help clarify questions
8. Practice, practice, practice
9. Get a good night's sleep; don't try to cram the night before the test
10. Eat a well balanced meal
11. Know the exact physical location of the testing site; drive the route to the site prior to test day
12. Bring a set of ear plugs; the testing center could be noisy
13. Wear comfortable, loose fitting, layered clothing to the testing center; prepare for it to be either cold or hot during the test
14. Bring at least 2 current forms of ID to the testing center
15. Arrive to the test early; be prepared to wait and be patient
16. Eliminate the obviously wrong answer choices, then guess the first remaining choice
17. Pace yourself; don't rush, but keep working and move on if you get stuck
18. Maintain a positive attitude even if the test is going poorly
19. Keep your first answer unless you are positive it is wrong
20. Check your work, don't make a careless mistake

General Strategies

The most important thing you can do is to ignore your fears and jump into the test immediately- do not be overwhelmed by any strange-sounding terms. You have to jump into the test like jumping into a pool- all at once is the easiest way.

Make Predictions

As you read and understand the question, try to guess what the answer will be. Remember that several of the answer choices are wrong, and once you begin reading them, your mind will immediately become cluttered with answer choices designed to throw you off. Your mind is typically the most focused immediately after you have read the question and digested its contents. If you can, try to predict what the correct answer will be. You may be surprised at what you can predict.

Quickly scan the choices and see if your prediction is in the listed answer choices. If it is, then you can be quite confident that you have the right answer. It still won't hurt to check the other answer choices, but most of the time, you've got it!

Answer the Question

It may seem obvious to only pick answer choices that answer the question, but the test writers can create some excellent answer choices that are wrong. Don't pick an answer just because it sounds right, or you believe it to be true. It MUST answer the question. Once you've made your selection, always go back and check it against the question and make sure that you didn't misread the question, and the answer choice does answer the question posed.

Benchmark

After you read the first answer choice, decide if you think it sounds correct or not. If it doesn't, move on to the next answer choice. If it does, mentally mark that answer choice. This doesn't mean that you've definitely selected it as your answer choice, it just means that it's the best you've seen thus far. Go ahead and read the next choice. If the next choice is worse than the one you've already selected, keep going to the next answer choice. If the next choice is better than the choice you've already selected, mentally mark the new answer choice as your best guess.

The first answer choice that you select becomes your standard. Every other answer choice must be benchmarked against that standard. That choice is correct until proven otherwise by another answer choice beating it out. Once you've decided that no other answer choice seems as good, do one final check to ensure that your answer choice answers the question posed.

Valid Information

Don't discount any of the information provided in the question. Every piece of information may be necessary to determine the correct answer. None of the information in the question is there to throw you off (while the answer choices will certainly have information to throw you off). If two seemingly unrelated topics are discussed, don't ignore either. You can be confident there is a relationship, or it wouldn't be included in the question, and you are probably going to have to determine what is that relationship to find the answer.

Avoid "Fact Traps"

Don't get distracted by a choice that is factually true. Your search is for the answer that answers the question. Stay focused and don't fall for an answer that is true but incorrect. Always go back to the question and make sure you're choosing an answer that actually answers the question and is not just a true statement. An answer can be factually correct, but it MUST answer the question asked. Additionally, two answers can both be seemingly correct, so be sure to read all of the answer choices, and make sure that you get the one that BEST answers the question.

Milk the Question

Some of the questions may throw you completely off. They might deal with a subject you have not been exposed to, or one that you haven't reviewed in years. While your lack of knowledge about the subject will be a hindrance, the question itself can give you many clues that will help you find the correct answer. Read the question carefully and look for clues. Watch particularly for adjectives and nouns describing difficult terms or words that you don't recognize. Regardless of if you completely understand a word or not, replacing it with a synonym either provided or one you more familiar with may help you to understand what the questions are asking. Rather than wracking your mind about specific detailed information concerning a difficult term or word, try to use mental substitutes that are easier to understand.

The Trap of Familiarity

Don't just choose a word because you recognize it. On difficult questions, you may not recognize a number of words in the answer choices. The test writers don't put "make-believe" words on the test; so don't think that just because you only recognize all the words in one answer choice means that answer choice must be correct. If you only recognize words in one answer choice, then focus on that one. Is it correct? Try your best to determine if it is correct. If it is, that is great, but if it doesn't, eliminate it. Each word and answer choice you eliminate increases your chances of getting the question correct, even if you then have to guess among the

- 18 -

unfamiliar choices.

Eliminate Answers

Eliminate choices as soon as you realize they are wrong. But be careful! Make sure you consider all of the possible answer choices. Just because one appears right, doesn't mean that the next one won't be even better! The test writers will usually put more than one good answer choice for every question, so read all of them. Don't worry if you are stuck between two that seem right. By getting down to just two remaining possible choices, your odds are now 50/50. Rather than wasting too much time, play the odds. You are guessing, but guessing wisely, because you've been able to knock out some of the answer choices that you know are wrong. If you are eliminating choices and realize that the last answer choice you are left with is also obviously wrong, don't panic. Start over and consider each choice again. There may easily be something that you missed the first time and will realize on the second pass.

Tough Questions

If you are stumped on a problem or it appears too hard or too difficult, don't waste time. Move on! Remember though, if you can quickly check for obviously incorrect answer choices, your chances of guessing correctly are greatly improved. Before you completely give up, at least try to knock out a couple of possible answers. Eliminate what you can and then guess at the remaining answer choices before moving on.

Brainstorm

If you get stuck on a difficult question, spend a few seconds quickly brainstorming. Run through the complete list of possible answer choices. Look at each choice and ask yourself, "Could this answer the question satisfactorily?" Go through each answer choice and consider it independently of the other. By systematically going through all possibilities, you may find something that you would otherwise overlook. Remember that when you get stuck, it's important to try to keep moving.

Read Carefully

Understand the problem. Read the question and answer choices carefully. Don't miss the question because you misread the terms. You have plenty of time to read each question thoroughly and make sure you understand what is being asked. Yet a happy medium must be attained, so don't waste too much time. You must read carefully, but efficiently.

Face Value

When in doubt, use common sense. Always accept the situation in the problem at face value. Don't read too much into it. These problems will not require you to make huge leaps of logic. The test writers aren't trying to throw you off with a cheap trick. If you have to go beyond creativity and make a leap of logic in order to have an answer choice answer the question, then you should look at the other answer choices. Don't overcomplicate the problem by creating theoretical relationships or explanations that will warp time or space. These are normal problems rooted in reality. It's just that the applicable relationship or explanation may not be readily apparent and you have to figure things out. Use your common sense to interpret anything that isn't clear.

Prefixes

If you're having trouble with a word in the question or answer choices, try dissecting it. Take advantage of every clue that the word might include. Prefixes and suffixes can be a huge help. Usually they allow you to determine a basic meaning. Pre- means before, post- means after, pro - is positive, de- is negative. From these prefixes and suffixes, you can get an idea of the general meaning of the word and try to put it into context. Beware though of any traps. Just because con is the opposite of pro, doesn't necessarily mean congress is the opposite of progress!

Hedge Phrases

Watch out for critical "hedge" phrases, such as likely, may, can, will often, sometimes, often, almost, mostly, usually, generally, rarely, sometimes. Question writers insert these hedge phrases to cover every possibility. Often an answer choice will be wrong simply because it leaves no room for exception. Avoid answer choices that have definitive words like "exactly," and "always".

Switchback Words

Stay alert for "switchbacks". These are the words and phrases frequently used to alert you to shifts in thought. The most common switchback word is "but". Others include although, however, nevertheless, on the other hand, even though, while, in spite of, despite, regardless of.

New Information

Correct answer choices will rarely have completely new information included. Answer choices typically are straightforward reflections of the material asked about and will directly relate to the question. If a new piece of information is included in an answer choice that doesn't even seem to relate to the topic being asked about, then that answer choice is likely incorrect. All of the information needed to answer the question is usually provided for you, and so you should not have to make guesses that are unsupported or choose answer choices that require unknown information that cannot be reasoned on its own.

Time Management

On technical questions, don't get lost on the technical terms. Don't spend too much time on any one question. If you don't know what a term means, then since you don't have a dictionary, odds are you aren't going to get much further. You should immediately recognize terms as whether or not you know them. If you don't, work with the other clues that you have, the other answer choices and terms provided, but don't waste too much time trying to figure out a difficult term.

Contextual Clues

Look for contextual clues. An answer can be right but not correct. The contextual clues will help you find the answer that is most right and is correct. Understand the context in which a phrase or statement is made. This will help you make important distinctions.

Don't Panic

Panicking will not answer any questions for you. Therefore, it isn't helpful. When you first see the question, if your mind goes blank, take a deep breath. Force yourself to mechanically go through the steps of solving the problem and using the strategies you've learned.

Pace Yourself

Don't get clock fever. It's easy to be overwhelmed when you're looking at a page full of questions, your mind is full of random thoughts and feeling confused, and the clock is ticking down faster than you would like. Calm down and maintain the pace that you have set for yourself. As long as you are on track by monitoring your pace, you are guaranteed to have enough time for yourself. When you get to the last few minutes of the test, it may seem like you won't have enough time left, but if you only have as many questions as you should have left at that point, then you're right on track!

Answer Selection

The best way to pick an answer choice is to eliminate all of those that are wrong, until only one is left and confirm that is the correct answer. Sometimes though, an answer choice may immediately look right. Be careful! Take a second to make sure that the other choices are not equally obvious. Don't make a hasty mistake. There are only two times that you should stop before checking other answers. First is when you are positive that the answer choice you have selected is correct. Second is when time is almost out and you have to make a quick guess!

Check Your Work

Since you will probably not know every term listed and the answer to every question, it is important that you get credit for the ones that you do know. Don't miss any questions through careless mistakes. If at all possible, try to take a second to look back over your answer selection and make sure you've selected the correct answer choice and haven't made a costly careless mistake (such as marking an answer choice that you didn't mean to mark). This quick double check should more than pay for itself in caught mistakes for the time it costs.

Beware of Directly Quoted Answers

Sometimes an answer choice will repeat word for word a portion of the question or reference section. However, beware of such exact duplication – it may be a trap!

More than likely, the correct choice will paraphrase or summarize a point, rather than being exactly the same wording.

Slang

Scientific sounding answers are better than slang ones. An answer choice that begins "To compare the outcomes…" is much more likely to be correct than one that begins "Because some people insisted…"

Extreme Statements

Avoid wild answers that throw out highly controversial ideas that are proclaimed as established fact. An answer choice that states the "process should used in certain situations, if…" is much more likely to be correct than one that states the "process should be discontinued completely." The first is a calm rational statement and doesn't even make a definitive, uncompromising stance, using a hedge word "if" to provide wiggle room, whereas the second choice is a radical idea and far more extreme.

Answer Choice Families

When you have two or more answer choices that are direct opposites or parallels, one of them is usually the correct answer. For instance, if one answer choice states "x increases" and another answer choice states "x decreases" or "y increases," then those two or three answer choices are very similar in construction and fall into the same family of answer choices. A family of answer choices is when two or three answer choices are very similar in construction, and yet often have a directly opposite meaning. Usually the correct answer choice will be in that family of answer choices. The "odd man out" or answer choice that doesn't seem to fit the parallel construction of the other answer choices is more likely to be incorrect.

Mathematics Test

A detailed knowledge of algebra and trigonometry is NOT necessary to answer to succeed on MCAS Mathematical test. Don't be intimidated by the questions presented. They do not require highly advanced math knowledge, but only the ability to recognize basic problems types and apply simple formulas and methods to solving them.

That is our goal, to show you the simple formulas and methods to solving these problems, so that while you will not gain a mastery of math from this guide, you will learn the methods necessary to succeed on the MCAS. This guide attacks problems that are simple in nature but may have been glossed over during your education.

- All numbers used are real numbers.
- Figures or drawings beside questions are provided as additional information that should be useful in solving the problem. They are drawn fairly accurately, unless the figure is noted as "not drawn to scale".
- Jagged or straight lines can both be assumed to be straight.
- Unless otherwise stated, all drawings and figures lie in a plane.

Solving for Variables

Variables are letters that represent an unknown number. You must solve for that unknown number in single variable problems. The main thing to remember is that you can do anything to one side of an equation as long as you do it to the other.

Example: Solve for x in the equation $2x + 3 = 5$.

Answer: First you want to get the "2x" isolated by itself on one side. To do that, first get rid of the 3. Subtract 3 from both sides of the equation $2x + 3 - 3 = 5 - 3$ or $2x =$

2. Now since the x is being multiplied by the 2 in "2x", you must divide by 2 to get rid of it. So, divide both sides by 2, which gives 2x / 2 = 2 / 2 or x = 1.

Drawings

Other problems may describe a geometric shape, such as a triangle or circle, but may not include a drawing of the shape. MCAS is testing whether you can read a description and make appropriate inferences by visualizing the object and related information. There is a simple way to overcome this obstacle. DRAW THE SHAPE! A good drawing (or even a bad drawing) is much easier to understand and interpret than a brief description.

Make a quick drawing or sketch of the shape described. Include any angles or lengths provided in the description. Once you can see the shape, you have already partially solved the problem and will be able to determine the right answer.

Positive/Negative Numbers

Multiplication/Division

A negative multiplied or divided by a negative = a positive number.

Example: -3 * -4 = 12; -6 / -3 = 2

A negative multiplied by a positive = a negative number.

Example: -3 * 4 = -12; -6 / 3 = -2

Addition/Subtraction

Treat a negative sign just like a subtraction sign.

Example: 3 + -2 = 3 – 2 or 1

Remember that you can reverse the numbers while adding or subtracting.

Example: -4+2 = 2 + -4 = 2 – 4 = -2

A negative number subtracted from another number is the same as adding a positive number.

Example: 2 - -1 = 2 + 1 = 3

Beware of making a simple mistake!

Example: An outdoor thermometer drops from 42º to – 8º. By how many degrees has the outside air cooled?

Answer: A common mistake is to say 42º – 8º = 34º, but that is wrong. It is actually 42º - - 8º or 42º + 8º = 50º

Exponents

When exponents are multiplied together, the exponents are added to get the final result.

Example: $x*x = x^2$, where x^1 is implied and $1 + 1 = 2$.

When exponents in parentheses have an exponent, the exponents are multiplied to get the final result.

Example: $(x^3)^2 = x^6$, because $3*2 = 6$.

Another way to think of this is that $(x^3)^2$ is the same as $(x^3)*(x^3)$. Now you can use the multiplication rule given above and add the exponents, $3 + 3 = 6$, so $(x^3)^2 = x^6$

Decimal Exponents (aka Scientific Notation)

This usually involves converting back and forth between scientific notation and decimal numbers (e.g. 0.02 is the same as 2×10^{-2}). There's an old "cheat" to this problem: if the number is less than 1, the number of digits behind the decimal point is the same as the exponent that 10 is raised to in scientific notation, except that the exponent is a negative number; if the number is greater than 1, the exponent of 10 is equal to the number of digits ahead of the decimal point minus 1.

Example: Convert 3000 to decimal notation.

Answer: 3×10^3, since 4 digits are ahead of the decimal, the number is greater than 1, and (4-1) = 3.

Example: Convert 0.05 to decimal notation.

Answer: 5 x 10⁻², since the five is two places behind the decimal (remember, the exponent is negative for numbers less than 1).

Any number raised to an exponent of zero is always 1. Also, unless you know what you're doing, always convert scientific notation to "regular" decimal numbers before doing arithmetic, and convert the answer back if necessary to answer the problem.

Area, Volume, and Surface Area

You can count on questions about area, volume, and surface area to be a significant part of the MCAS. While commonly used formulas are provided in the actual MCAS test book, it is best to become familiar with the formulas beforehand. A list is provided in the appendix for your convenience.

Percents

A percent can be converted to a decimal simply by dividing it by 100.

Example: What is 2% of 50?

Answer: 2% = 2/100 or .02, so .02 * 50 = 1

Word Problems

Percents

Example: Ticket sales for this year's annual concert at Minutemaid Park were $125,000. The promoter is predicting that next year's sales, in dollars, will be 40% greater than this year's. How many dollars in ticket sales is the promoter predicting for next year?

Answer: Next year's is 40% greater. 40% = 40/100 = .4, so .4 * $125,000 = $50,000. However, the example stated that next year's would be greater by that amount, so next year's sales would be this year's at $125,000 plus the increase at $50,000.

$125,000 + $50,000 = $175,000

Distances

Example: In a certain triangle, the longest side is 1 foot longer than the second-longest side, and the second-longest side is 1 foot longer than the shortest side. If the perimeter is 30 feet, how many feet long is the shortest side.

Answer: There are three sides, let's call them A, B, and C. A is the longest, B the medium sized, and C the shortest. Because A is described in reference to B's length and B is described in reference to C's length, all calculations should be done off of C, the final reference. Use a variable to represent C's length, "x". This means that C is "x" long, B is "x + 1" because B was 1 foot longer than C, and A is "x + 1 + 1" because A was 1 foot longer than B. To calculate a perimeter you simply add all three sides together, so P = length A + length B + length C, or (x) + (x + 1) + (x + 1 + 1) = x + x + x + 1 + 1 + 1 = 3x + 3. You know that the perimeter equals 30 feet, so 3x + 3 = 30. Subtracting 3 from both sides gives 3x + 3 – 3 = 30 – 3 or 3x = 27. Dividing both sides by 3 to get "x" all by itself gives 3x / 3 = 27 / 3 or x = 9. So C = x = 9, and B = x + 1 = 9 + 1 = 10, and A = x + 1 + 1 = 9 + 1 + 1 = 11. A quick check of 9 + 10 + 11 = 30 for the perimeter distance proves that the answer of x = 9 is correct

Ratios

Example: An architect is drawing a scaled blueprint of an apartment building that is to be 100 feet wide and 250 feet long. On the drawing, if the building is 25 inches long, how many inches wide should it be?

Answer: Recognize the word "scaled" to indicate a similar drawing. Similar drawings or shapes can be solved using ratios. First, create the ratio fraction for the missing number, in this case the number of inches wide the drawing should be. The numerator of the first ratio fraction will be the matching known side, in this case "100 feet" wide. The question "100 feet wide is to how many inches wide?" gives us the first fraction of 100 / x. The question "250 feet long is to 25 inches long?" gives us the second fraction of 250 / 25. Again, note that both numerators (100 and 250) are from the same shape. The denominators ("x" and 25) are both from the same shape or drawing as well. Cross multiplication gives 100 * 25 = 250 * x or 2500 = 250x. Dividing both sides by 250 to get x by itself yields 2500 / 250 = 250x / 250 or 10 = x.

Special Formulas

FOIL (First, Outer, Inner, Last)

When you are given a problem such as $(x + 2)(x - 3)$, you should use the FOIL method of multiplication. First, multiply the First parts of each equation $(x*x)$. Then multiply the Outer parts of each equation $(x*-3)$. Note that you should treat the minus 3 in the second equation as a negative 3. Then multiply the Inner parts of each equation $(2*x)$. Finally, multiply the Last parts of each equation $(2*-3)$. Once you are finished, add each part together $(x*x)+(x*-3)+(2*x)+(2*-3) = x^2 + -3x + 2x + -6 = x^2 - 3x + 2x - 6 = x^2 - 1x - 6 = x^2 - x - 6$.

Slope-Intercept formula

$y = mx + b$, where m is the slope of the line and b is the y-intercept.

Example: In the (x,y) coordinate plane, what is the slope of the line $2y = x - 4$?

Answer: First this needs to be converted into slope intercept form. Divide both sides by 2, which gives $2y/2 = (x-4)/2$ or $y = x/2 - 2$. $x/2$ is the same as $½ *x$, so since m in the formula $y = mx+b$ is the slope, then in the equation $y = ½ * x - 2$, $½$ is the slope.

Example: In the (x,y) coordinate plane, where does the line $y = 2x - 3$ cross the y-axis?

Answer: In the formula y = mx + b, b is the y – intercept, or where the line crosses the y-axis. In this case, b is represented by –3, so –3 is where the line crosses the y-axis.

Example: In the (x , y) coordinate plane, what is the slope of the line y = x + 2?

Answer: This is already in the slope intercept form of y = mx + b. Whenever x does not have a number in front of it, you can always assume that there is a 1 there. Therefore, this equation could also be written as y = 1x + 2, which means m = 1, and the slope is 1.

Slope formula

m = (y1 – y2)/(x1 – x2), where m is the slope of the line and two points on the line are given by (x1,y1) and (x2,y2). This can sometimes be remembered by the statement "rise over run", which means that the "y" values represent the "rise" as they are the up and down dimension and the "x" values represent the "run" as they are the side to side dimension.

Example: What is the slope of a line that passes through points (5,1) and (-2, 3).

Answer: m = (y1 – y2)/(x1 – x2) or (1 – 3)/(5 - -2) or –2 / (5 + 2) or –2 / 7

Line Plotting

If you are trying to plot a line, there is an easy way to do it. First convert the line into slope intercept form (y = mx + b). Then, put a dot on the y-axis at the value of b. For example, if you have a line given by y= 2/3x + 1, then the first point on the line would be at (0,1), because 1 is the y-intercept, or where the line crosses the y-axis. To find the next point on the line, use the slope, which is 2/3. First go 2 increments up, and then 3 increments to the right. To find the next point on the line, go 2 more increments up, and then 3 more increments to the right. You should always go either up or down depending on the numerator in the slope fraction. So if the slope is 3/5, then the numerator is 3, and you should go 3 increments up and 5 increments to the right. You should always go to the right the amount of the denominator. So if the slope is –2, then first you should remember that –2 is the same as –2/1. Since –2 is the numerator, you should go down 2 increments and then 1 increment to the right.

Remember that positive slopes slope upward from left to right and that negative slopes slope downward from left to right.

Simple Probability

The probability problems on the MCAS are fairly straightforward. The basic idea is this: the probability that something will happen is the number of possible ways that something can happen divided by the total number of possible ways for all things that can happen.

Example: I have 20 balloons, 12 are red, 8 are yellow. I give away one yellow balloon; if the next balloon is randomly picked, what is the probability that it will be yellow?

Answer: The probability is 7/19, because after giving one away, there are 7 different ways that the "something" can happen, divided by 19 remaining possibilities.

Ratios

When a question asks about two similar shapes, expect a ratio problem.

Example: The figure below shows 2 triangles, where triangle ABC ~ A'B'C'. In these similar triangles, a = 3, b = 4, c = 5, and a' = 6. What is the value of b'?

Answer: You are given the dimensions of 1 side that is similar on both triangles (a and a'). You are looking for b' and are given the dimensions of b. Therefore you can set up a ratio of a/a' = b/b' or 3/6 = 4/b'. To solve, cross multiply the two sides, multiplying 6*4 = 3*b' or 24 = 3b'. Dividing both sides by 3 (24/3 = 3b'/3) makes 8 = b', so 8 is the answer.

Note many other problems may have opportunities to use a ratio. Look for problems where you are trying to find dimensions for a shape and you have dimensions for a similar shape. These can nearly always be solved by setting up a ratio. Just be careful and set up corresponding measurements in the ratios. First decide what you are being asked for on shape B, represented by a variable, such as x. Then ask yourself, which side on similar shape A is the same size side as x. That is your first ratio fraction, set up a fraction like 2/x if 2 is the similar size side on shape A. Then find a side on each shape that is similar. If 4 is the size of another side on shape A and it corresponds to a side with size 3 on shape B, then your second ratio fraction is 4/3. Note that 2 and 4 are the two numerators in the ratio fractions and are both from shape A. Also note that "x" the unknown side and 3 are both the denominators in the ratio fractions and are both from shape B.

Graphs

Midpoints

To find a midpoint, find the difference in the x-direction between the two endpoints given, and divide by two. Then add that number to the leftmost endpoint's x coordinate. That will be the x coordinate of the midpoint. Next find the difference in the y-direction between the two endpoints given, and divide by two. Then add that number to the lower endpoint's y coordinate. That will be the y coordinate of the midpoint.

Example: What is the midpoint of the line segment with endpoints of (-2 , 5) and (4 , 1)?

Answer: First, subtract the leftmost endpoint's x coordinate from the rightmost endpoint's x coordinate 4 - -2 = 4 + 2 = 6. Then divide by two, 6 / 2 = 3. Then add that number to the leftmost x coordinate -2 + 3 = 1, which is the midpoint's x coordinate. Second, subtract the lower endpoint's y coordinate from the higher endpoint's y coordinate 5 - 1 = 4. Then divide by two, 4 / 2 = 2. Then add that number to the lower y coordinate 1 + 2 = 3, which is the midpoint's y coordinate. So the midpoint is given by (1 , 3).

Angles

If you have a two intersecting lines, remember that the sum of all of the angles can only be 360°. In fact, the two angles on either side of each line will add up to 180°. In the example below, on either side of each line, there is a 137° angle and a 43° angle (137° + 43°) = 180°. Also note that opposite angles are equal. For example, the 43° angle is matched by a similar 43° angle on the opposite side of the intersection.

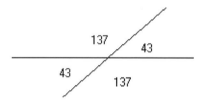

Additionally, parallel lines intersected by a third line will share angles. In the example below, note how each 128° angle is matched by a 128° angle on the opposite side. Also, all of the other angles in this example are 52° angles, because all of the angles on one side of a line have to equal 180° and since there are only two angles, if you have the degree of one, then you can find the degree of the other. In this case, the missing angle is given by 180° − 128° = 52°.

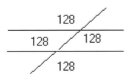

Finally, remember that all of the angles in a triangle will add up to 180°. If you are given two of the angles, then subtract them both from 180° and you will have the degree of the third missing angle.

Example: If you have a triangle with two given angles of 20° and 130°, what degree is the third angle?

Answer: All angles must add up to 180°, so 180° − 20° − 130° = 30°.

Right Triangles

Whenever you see the words "right triangle" or "90° angle," alarm bells should go off. These problems will almost always involve the law of right triangles, AKA The Pythagorean Theorem:

$A^2 + B^2 = C^2$

Where A = the length of one of the shorter sides

B = the length of the other shorter side

C = the length of the hypotenuse or longest side opposite the 90° angle

MAKE SURE YOU KNOW THIS FORMULA. At least 3-5 questions will reference variations on this formula by giving you two of the three variables and asking you to solve for the third.

Example: A right triangle has sides of 3 and 4; what is the length of the hypotenuse?

Answer: Solving the equation, $A^2=9$, $B^2=16$, so $C^2=25$; the square root of 25 is 5, the length of the hypotenuse C.

Example: In the rectangle below, what is the length of the diagonal line?

Answer: This rectangle is actually made of two right triangles. Whenever you have a right triangle, the Pythagorean Theorem can be used. Since the right side of the triangle is equal to 5, then the left side must also be equal to 5. This creates a triangle with one side equal to 5 and another side equal to 8. To use the Pythagorean Theorem, we state that $5^2 + 8^2 = C^2$ or $25 + 64 = C^2$ or $89 = C^2$ or C = Square Root of 89

Circles

Many test takers have never seen the formula for a circle:

$(x-A)^2 + (y-B)^2 = r^2$

This looks intimidating, but it's really not:

A = the coordinate of the center on the x-axis

B = the coordinate of the center on the y-axis

r = the radius of the circle

Example: What is the radius of the circle described by: $(x+2)^2 + (x-3)^2 = 16$

Answer: Since $r^2 = 16$, r, the radius, equals 4.

Also, this circle is centered at (-2,3) since those must be the values of A and B in the generic equation to make it the same as this equation.

Final Note

As mentioned before, word problems describing shapes should always be drawn out. Remember the old adage that a picture is worth a thousand words. If geometric shapes are described (line segments, circles, squares, etc) draw them out rather than trying to visualize how they should look.

Approach problems systematically. Take time to understand what is being asked for. In many cases there is a drawing or graph that you can write on. Draw lines, jot notes, do whatever is necessary to create a visual picture and to allow you to understand what is being asked.

Even if you have always done well in math, you may not succeed on the MCAS. While normal math tests in school test specific competencies in specific subjects, the MCAS frequently tests your ability to apply math concepts from vastly different math subjects in one problem. However, in few cases is any MCAS Mathematics problem more than two "layers" deep.

What does this mean for you? You can easily learn the MCAS Mathematics through taking multiple practice tests. If you have some gaps in your math knowledge, we suggest you buy a more basic study guide to help you build a foundation before applying our secrets. Check out our special report to find out which books are worth your time.

English Language Arts
Language and Literature Test

Skimming

Your first task when you begin reading is to answer the question "What is the topic of the selection?" This can best be answered by quickly skimming the passage for the general idea, stopping to read only the first sentence of each paragraph. A paragraph's first sentence is usually the main topic sentence, and it gives you a summary of the content of the paragraph.

Once you've skimmed the passage, stopping to read only the first sentences, you will have a general idea about what it is about, as well as what is the expected topic in each paragraph.

Each question will contain clues as to where to find the answer in the passage. Do not just randomly search through the passage for the correct answer to each question. Search scientifically. Find key word(s) or ideas in the question that are going to either contain or be near the correct answer. These are typically nouns, verbs, numbers, or phrases in the question that will probably be duplicated in the passage. Once you have identified those key word(s) or idea, skim the passage quickly to find where those key word(s) or idea appears. The correct answer choice will be nearby.

Example: What caused Martin to suddenly return to Paris?

The key word is Paris. Skim the passage quickly to find where this word appears. The answer will be close by that word.

However, sometimes key words in the question are not repeated in the passage. In those cases, search for the general idea of the question.

Example: Which of the following was the psychological impact of the author's childhood upon the remainder of his life?

Key words are "childhood" or "psychology". While searching for those words, be alert for other words or phrases that have similar meaning, such as "emotional effect" or "mentally" which could be used in the passage, rather than the exact word "psychology".

Numbers or years can be particularly good key words to skim for, as they stand out from the rest of the text.

Example: Which of the following best describes the influence of Monet's work in the 20th century?

20th contains numbers and will easily stand out from the rest of the text. Use 20th as the key word to skim for in the passage.

Other good key word(s) may be in quotation marks. These identify a word or phrase that is copied directly from the passage. In those cases, the word(s) in quotation marks are exactly duplicated in the passage.

Example: In her college years, what was meant by Margaret's "drive for excellence"?

"Drive for excellence" is a direct quote from the passage and should be easy to find.

Once you've quickly found the correct section of the passage to find the answer, focus upon the answer choices. Sometimes a choice will repeat word for word a portion of the passage near the answer. However, beware of such duplication – it may be a trap! More than likely, the correct choice will paraphrase or summarize the related portion of the passage, rather than being exactly the same wording.

For the answers that you think are correct, read them carefully and make sure that they answer the question. An answer can be factually correct, but it MUST answer the question asked. Additionally, two answers can both be seemingly correct, so be sure to read all of the answer choices, and make sure that you get the one that BEST answers the question.

Some questions will not have a key word.

Example: Which of the following would the author of this passage likely agree with?

In these cases, look for key words in the answer choices. Then skim the passage to find where the answer choice occurs. By skimming to find where to look, you can minimize the time required.

Sometimes it may be difficult to identify a good key word in the question to skim for in the passage. In those cases, look for a key word in one of the answer choices to skim for. Often the answer choices can all be found in the same paragraph, which can quickly narrow your search.

Paragraph Focus

Focus upon the first sentence of each paragraph, which is the most important. The main topic of the paragraph is usually there.

Once you've read the first sentence in the paragraph, you have a general idea about what each paragraph will be about. As you read the questions, try to determine which paragraph will have the answer. Paragraphs have a concise topic. The answer should either obviously be there or obviously not. It will save time if you can jump straight to the paragraph, so try to remember what you learned from the first sentences.

Example: The first paragraph is about poets; the second is about poetry. If a question asks about poetry, where will the answer be? The second paragraph.

The main idea of a passage is typically spread across all or most of its paragraphs. Whereas the main idea of a paragraph may be completely different than the main idea of the very next paragraph, a main idea for a passage affects all of the paragraphs in one form or another.

Example: What is the main idea of the passage?

For each answer choice, try to see how many paragraphs are related. It can help to count how many sentences are affected by each choice, but it is best to see how many paragraphs are affected by the choice. Typically the answer choices will include incorrect choices that are main ideas of individual paragraphs, but not the entire passage. That is why it is crucial to choose ideas that are supported by the most paragraphs possible.

Eliminate Choices

Some choices can quickly be eliminated. "Andy Warhol lived there." Is Andy Warhol even mentioned in the article? If not, quickly eliminate it.

When trying to answer a question such as "the passage indicates all of the following EXCEPT" quickly skim the paragraph searching for references to each choice. If the reference exists, scratch it off as a choice. Similar choices may be crossed off simultaneously if they are close enough.

In choices that ask you to choose "which answer choice does NOT describe?" or "all of the following answer choices are identifiable characteristics, EXCEPT which?" look for answers that are similarly worded. Since only one answer can be correct, if there are two answers that appear to mean the same thing, they must BOTH be incorrect, and can be eliminated.

Example:

A.)   changing values and attitudes

B.)   a large population of mobile or uprooted people

These answer choices are similar; they both describe a fluid culture. Because of their similarity, they can be linked together. Since the answer can have only one choice, they can also be eliminated together.

When presented with a question that offers two choices, or neither choice, or both choice, it is rarely both choices.

Example: When an atom emits a beta particle, the mass of the atom will:

A.   increase

B.   decrease.

C.   stay the same.

D.   either increase or decrease depending on conditions.

Answer D will rarely be correct, the answers are usually more concrete.

Contextual Clues

Look for contextual clues. An answer can be right but not correct. The contextual clues will help you find the answer that is most right and is correct. Understand the context in which a phrase is stated.

When asked for the implied meaning of a statement made in the passage, immediately go find the statement and read the context it was made in. Also, look for an answer choice that has a similar phrase to the statement in question. Example: In the passage, what is implied by the phrase "Churches have become more or less part of the furniture"?

Find an answer choice that is similar or describes the phrase "part of the furniture" as that is the key phrase in the question. "Part of the furniture" is a saying that means something is fixed, immovable, or set in their ways. Those are all similar ways of saying "part of the furniture." As such, the correct answer choice will probably include a similar rewording of the expression.
Example: Why was John described as "morally desperate".

The answer will probably have some sort of definition of morals in it. "Morals" refers to a code of right and wrong behavior, so the correct answer choice will likely have words that mean something like that.

Fact/Opinion

When asked about which statement is a fact or opinion, remember that answer choices that are facts will typically have no ambiguous words. For example, how long is a long time? What defines an ordinary person? These ambiguous words of "long" and "ordinary" should not be in a factual statement. However, if all of the choices have ambiguous words, go to the context of the passage. Often a factual statement may be set out as a research finding.
Example: "The scientist found that the eye reacts quickly to change in light."

Opinions may be set out in the context of words like thought, believed, understood, or wished.
Example: "He thought the Yankees should win the World Series."

Opposites

Answer choices that are direct opposites are usually correct. The paragraph will often contain established relationships (when this goes up, that goes down). The question may ask you to draw conclusions for this and will give two similar answer choices that are opposites.

Example:

A.) if other factors are held constant, then increasing the interest rate will lead to a decrease in housing starts

B.) if other factors are held constant, then increasing the interest rate will lead to an increase in housing starts

Often these opposites will not be so clearly recognized. Don't be thrown off by different wording, look for the meaning beneath. Notice how these two answer choices are really opposites, with just a slight change in the wording shown above. Once you realize these are opposites, you should examine them closely. One of these two is likely to be the correct answer.

Example:

A.) if other factors are held constant, then increasing the interest rate will lead to a decrease in housing starts

B.) when there is an increase in housing starts, and other things remaining equal, it is often the result of an increase in interest rates

Make Predictions

As you read and understand the passage and then the question, try to guess what the answer will be. Remember that three of the four answer choices are wrong, and once you being reading them, your mind will immediately become cluttered with answer choices designed to throw you off. Your mind is typically the most focused immediately after you have read the passage and question and digested its contents. If you can, try to predict what the correct answer will be. You may be surprised at what you can predict.

Quickly scan the choices and see if your prediction is in the listed answer choices. If it is, then you can be quite confident that you have the right answer. It still won't hurt to check the other answer choices, but most of the time, you've got it!

Answer the Question

It may seem obvious to only pick answer choices that answer the question, but MCAS can create some excellent answer choices that are wrong. Don't pick an answer just because it sounds right, or you believe it to be true. It MUST answer the question. Once you've made your selection, always go back and check it against the question and make sure that you didn't misread the question, and the answer choice does answer the question posed.

Benchmark

After you read the first answer choice, decide if you think it sounds correct or not. If it doesn't, move on to the next answer choice. If it does, make a mental note about that choice. This doesn't mean that you've definitely selected it as your answer choice, it just means that it's the best you've seen thus far. Go ahead and read the next choice. If the next choice is worse than the one you've already selected, keep going to the next answer choice. If the next choice is better than the choice you've already selected, then make a mental note about that answer choice.

As you read through the list, you are mentally noting the choice you think is right. That is your new standard. Every other answer choice must be benchmarked against that standard. That choice is correct until proven otherwise by another

- 45 -

answer choice beating it out. Once you've decided that no other answer choice seems as good, do one final check to ensure that it answers the question posed.

New Information

Correct answers will usually contain the information listed in the paragraph and question. Rarely will completely new information be inserted into a correct answer choice. Occasionally the new information may be related in a manner that MCAS is asking for you to interpret, but seldom.

Example:

The argument above is dependent upon which of the following assumptions?

A.) Scientists have used Charles's Law to interpret the relationship.

If Charles's Law is not mentioned at all in the referenced paragraph and argument, then it is unlikely that this choice is correct. All of the information needed to answer the question is provided for you, and so you should not have to make guesses that are unsupported or choose answer choices that have unknown information that cannot be reasoned.

Key Words

Look for answer choices that have the same key words in them as the question.

Example:

Which of the following, if true, would best explain the reluctance of politicians since 1980 to support this funding?

Look for the key words "since 1980" to be referenced in the correct answer choice. Most valid answer choices would probably include a phrase such as "since 1980, politicians have..."

Valid Information

Don't discount any of the information provided in the passage, particularly shorter ones. Every piece of information may be necessary to determine the correct answer. None of the information in the paragraph is there to throw you off (while the answer choices will certainly have information to throw you off). If two seemingly unrelated topics are discussed, don't ignore either. You can be confident there is a relationship, or it wouldn't be included in the paragraph, and you are probably going to have to determine what is that relationship for the answer.

Time Management

In technical passages, do not get lost on the technical terms. Skip them and move on. You want a general understanding of what is going on, not a mastery of the passage.

When you encounter material in the selection that seems difficult to understand, it often may not be necessary and can be skipped. Only spend time trying to understand it if it is going to be relevant for a question. Understand difficult phrases only as a last resort.

Answer general questions before detail questions. A reader with a good understanding of the whole passage can often answer general questions without rereading a word. Get the easier questions out of the way before tackling the more time consuming ones.

Identify each question by type. Usually the wording of a question will tell you whether you can find the answer by referring directly to the passage or by using your reasoning powers. You alone know which question types you customarily handle with ease and which give you trouble and will require more time. Save the difficult questions for last.

Final Warnings

Hedge Phrases Revisited

Once again, watch out for critical "hedge" phrases, such as likely, may, can, will often, sometimes, etc, often, almost, mostly, usually, generally, rarely, sometimes. Question writers insert these hedge phrases, to cover every possibility. Often an answer will be wrong simply because it leaves no room for exception.
Example: Animals live longer in cold places than animals in warm places.

This answer choice is wrong, because there are exceptions in which certain warm climate animals live longer. This answer choice leaves no possibility of exception. It states that every animal species in cold places live longer than animal species in warm places. Correct answer choices will typically have a key hedge word to leave room for exceptions.
Example: In severe cold, a polar bear cub is likely to survive longer than an adult polar bear.

This answer choice is correct, because not only does the passage imply that younger animals survive better in the cold, it also allows for exceptions to exist. The use of the word "likely" leaves room for cases in which a polar bear cub might not survive longer than the adult polar bear.

Word Usage Questions

When asked how a word is used in the passage, don't use your existing knowledge of the word. The question is being asked precisely because there is some strange or unusual usage of the word in the passage. Go to the passage and use contextual clues to determine the answer. Don't simply use the popular definition you already know.

Switchback Words

Stay alert for "switchbacks". These are the words and phrases frequently used to alert you to shifts in thought. The most common switchback word is "but". Others include although, however, nevertheless, on the other hand, even though, while, in spite of, despite, regardless of.

Avoid "Fact Traps"

Once you know which paragraph the answer will be in, focus on that paragraph. However, don't get distracted by a choice that is factually true about the paragraph. Your search is for the answer that answers the question, which may be about a tiny aspect in the paragraph. Stay focused and don't fall for an answer that describes the larger picture of the paragraph. Always go back to the question and make sure you're choosing an answer that actually answers the question and is not just a true statement.

English Language Arts Composition Test

A topic will be presented to you and you must write out a discussion on it. There is not a "correct" answer to the topic. You must evaluate the topic, organize your ideas, and develop them into a cohesive and coherent response.

You will be scored on how well you are able to utilize standard written English, organize and explain your thoughts, and support those thoughts with reasons and examples.

Brainstorm

Spend the first few minutes brainstorming out ideas. Write down any ideas you might have on the topic. The purpose is to extract from the recesses of your memory any relevant information. In this stage, anything goes down. Write down any idea, regardless of how good it may initially seem.

Strength through Diversity

The best papers will contain diversity of examples and reasoning. As you brainstorm consider different perspectives. Not only are there two sides to every issue, but there are also countless perspectives that can be considered. On any issue, different groups are impacted, with many reaching the same conclusion or position, but through vastly different paths. Try to "see" the issue through as many different eyes as you can. Look at it from every angle and from every vantage point. The more diverse the reasoning used, the more balanced the paper will become and the better the score.

Example:

The issue of free trade is not just two sided. It impacts politicians, domestic (US) manufacturers, foreign manufacturers, the US economy, the world economy, strategic alliances, retailers, wholesalers, consumers, unions, workers, and the exchange of more than just goods, but also of ideas, beliefs, and cultures. The more of these angles that you can approach the issue from, the more solid your reasoning and the stronger your position.

Furthermore, don't just use information as to how the issue impacts other people. Draw liberally from your own experience and your own observations. Explain a personal experience that you have had and your own emotions from that moment. Anything that you've seen in your community or observed in society can be expanded upon to further round out your position on the issue.

Pick a Main Idea

Once you have finished with your creative flow, stop and review it. Which idea were you able to come up with the most supporting information? It's extremely important that you pick an angle that will allow you to have a thorough and comprehensive coverage of the topic. This is not about your personal convictions, but about writing a concise rational discussion of an idea.

Weed the Garden

Every garden of ideas gets weeds in it. The ideas that you brainstormed over are going to be random pieces of information of mixed value. Go through it methodically and pick out the ones that are the best. The best ideas are strong points that it will be easy to write a few sentences or a paragraph about.

Create a Logical Flow

Now that you know which ideas you are going to use and focus upon, organize them. Put your writing points in a logical order. You have your main ideas that you will focus on, and must align them in a sequence that will flow in a smooth, sensible path from point to point, so that the reader will go smoothly from one idea to the next in a logical path. Readers must have a sense of continuity as they read your paper. You don't want to have a paper that rambles back and forth.

Start Your Engines

You have a logical flow of main ideas with which to start writing. Begin expanding on the issues in the sequence that you have set for yourself. Pace yourself. Don't spend too much time on any one of the ideas that you are expanding upon. You want to have spend the same amount of time on all of them.

Once you finish expanding on each idea, go back to your brainstorming session up above, where you wrote out your ideas. Go ahead and erase the ideas as you write about them. This will let you see what you need to write about next, and also allow you to pace yourself and see what you have left to cover.

First Paragraph

Your first paragraph should have several easily identifiable features.
- First, it should have a quick description or paraphrasing of the topic. Use your own words to briefly explain what the topic is about.
- Second, you should explain your opinion of the topic and give an explanation of why you feel that way. What is your decision or conclusion on the topic?
- Third, you should list your "writing points". What are the main ideas that you came up with earlier? This is your opportunity to outline the rest of your

paper. Have a sentence explaining each idea that you will go intend further depth in additional paragraphs. If someone was to only read this paragraph, they should be able to get an "executive summary" of the entire paper.

Body Paragraph

Each of your successive paragraphs should expand upon one of the points listed in the main paragraph. Use your personal experience and knowledge to support each of your points. Examples should back up everything.

Conclusion Paragraph

Once you have finished expanding upon each of your main points, wrap it up. Summarize what you have said and covered in a conclusion paragraph. Explain once more your opinion of the topic and quickly review why you feel that way. At this stage, you have already backed up your statements, so there is no need to do that again. All you are doing is refreshing in the mind of the reader the main points that you have made.

Don't Panic

Panicking will not put down any more words on paper for you. Therefore, it isn't helpful. When you first see the topic, if your mind goes as blank as the page on which you have to write out your paper, take a deep breath. Force yourself to mechanically go through the steps listed above.

Check Your Work

It is more important to have a shorter paper that is well written and well organized, than a longer paper that is poorly written and poorly organized. Don't keep writing about a subject just to add words and sentences, and certainly don't start repeating yourself. Expand on the ideas that you identified in the brainstorming session and make sure that you spend a few minutes at the end to go back and check your work.

At the end, go back and check over your work. Reread and make sure that everything you've written makes sense and flows. Clean up any spelling or grammar mistakes that you might have made. If you see anything that needs to be moved around, such as a paragraph that would fit in better somewhere else, cut and paste it to that new location. Also, go ahead and delete any brainstorming ideas that you weren't able to expand upon and clean up any other extraneous information that you might have written that doesn't fit into your paper.

As you proofread, make sure there aren't any fragments or run-ons. Check for sentences that are too short or too long. If the sentence is too short, look to see if you have an identifiable subject and verb. If it is too long, break it up into two separate sentences. Watch out for any "big" words you may have used. It's good to use difficult vocabulary words, but only if you are positive that you are using them correctly. Your paper has to be correct, it doesn't have to be fancy. You're not trying to impress anyone with your vocabulary, just your ability to develop and express ideas.

Final Note

Depending on your test taking preferences and personality, the essay writing will probably be your hardest or your easiest section. You are required to go through the entire process of writing a paper, which can be quite a challenge.

Focus upon each of the steps listed above. Go through the process of creative flow first, generating ideas and thoughts about the topic. Then organize those ideas into a smooth logical flow. Pick out the ones that are best from the list you have created. Decide which main idea or angle of the topic you will discuss.

Create a recognizable structure in your paper, with an introductory paragraph explaining what you have decided upon, and what your main points will be. Use the body paragraphs to expand on those main points and have a conclusion that wraps up the issue or topic.

Spend a few moments going back and reviewing what you have written. Clean up any minor mistakes that you might have had and give it those last few critical touches that can make a huge difference. Finally, be proud and confident of what you have written!

Special Report: Which MCAS Sample Questions Are Worth Your Time

We believe the following sample questions present uncommon value to our customers who wish to "really study" for the MCAS. While our manual teaches some valuable tricks and tips that no one else covers, going over the sample questions provided online is also helpful, though more time consuming.

Sample Questions

Official MCAS site:

http://www.doe.mass.edu/mcas/

This is a great source for REAL MCAS sample questions and information about the MCAS.

Special Report: What Your MCAS Score Means

The MCAS is a mechanism used to demonstrate that students have learned certain necessary academic skills in high school. Students must take the MCAS before they are able to receive their high school diplomas.

It is a pass/fail test that is not part of student's normal classwork. For students that are not able to pass the MCAS, they would still be eligible to take the GED, a high school equivalency exam, or to attend adult education classes to earn their diploma.

For most students passing the MCAS is a steppingstone to college and better things. In other words it may increase your lifetime earnings significantly and allow you to get that better paying job.

You can expect to achieve a salary increase of over $10,000-$20,000/year with the better paying job that your MCAS will enable you to achieve through paving the way for a college education. Once you have received your MCAS, by all means take the next step and attend an institution of higher learning. An education pays, and you should seek the maximum benefit of your efforts.

Special Report: MCAS Secrets in Action

Sample Question from the Mathematics Test

For a certain board game, two dice are thrown to determine the number of spaces to move. One player throws the two dice and the same number comes up on each of the dice. What is the probability that the sum of the two numbers is 9?

- 0
- 1/6
- 2/9
- 1/2

Let's look at a few different methods and steps to solving this problem.

1. Create an Algebra Problem

While you might think that creating an algebra problem is the last thing that you would want to do, it actually can make the problem extremely simple.

Consider what you know about the problem. You know that both dice are going to roll the same number, but you don't know what that number is. Therefore, make the number "x" the unknown variable that you will need to solve for.

Since you have two dice that both would roll the same number, then you have "2x" or "two times x". Since the sum of the two dice needs to equal nine, that gives you "2x = 9".

Solving for x, you should first divide both sides by 2. This creates $2x/2 = 9/2$. The twos cancel out on the left side and you are have $x = 9/2$ or $x = 4.5$

You know that a dice can only roll an integer: 1, 2, 3, 4, 5, or 6, therefore 4.5 is an impossible roll. An impossible roll means that there is a zero possibility it would occur, making choice A, zero, correct.

2. Run Through the Possibilities for Doubles

You know that you have to have the same number on both dice that you roll. There are only so many combinations, so quickly run through them all.

You could roll:

Double 1's = 1 + 1 = 2
Double 2's = 2 + 2 = 4
Double 3's = 3 + 3 = 6
Double 4's = 4 + 4 = 8
Double 5's = 5 + 5 = 10
Double 6's = 6 + 6 = 12

Now go through and see which, if any, combinations give you a sum of 9. As you can see here, there aren't any. No combination of doubles gives you a sum of 9, making it a zero probability, and choice A correct.

3. Run Through the Possibilities for Nine

Just as there are only so many possibilities for rolling doubles, there are also only so many possibilities to roll a sum of nine. Quickly calculate all the possibilities, starting with the first die.

If you rolled a 1 with the first die, then the highest you could roll with the second is a 6. Since 1 + 6 = 7, there is no way that you can roll a sum of 9 if your first die rolls a 1.

If you rolled a 2 with the first die, then the highest you could roll with the second is a 6. Since 2 + 6 = 8, there is no way that you can roll a sum of 9 if your first die rolls a 2.

If you rolled a 3 with the first die, then you could roll a 6 with your other die and have a sum of 9. Since 3 + 6 = 9, this is a valid possibility.

If you rolled a 4 with the first die, then you could roll a 5 with your other die and have a sum of 9. Since 4 + 5 = 9, this is a valid possibility.

If you rolled a 5 with the first die, then you could roll a 4 with your other die and have a sum of 9. Since 5 + 4 = 9, this is a valid possibility.

If you rolled a 6 with the first die, then you could roll a 3 with your other die and have a sum of 9. Since 6 + 3 = 9, this is a valid possibility.

Now review all the possibilities that give you a combination of 9. You have: 3 + 6, 4 + 5, 5 + 4, and 6 + 3. These are the only combinations that will give you a sum of 9, and none of them are doubles. Therefore, there is a zero probability that doubles could give you a sum of 9, and choice A is correct.

4. Calculate the Odds

Quickly calculate the odds for just rolling a 9, without setting any restrictions that it has to be through doubles or anything else. You've seen in Method 3 that there are 4 ways that you can roll a sum of 9. Since you have two dice, each with 6 sides, there are a total of 36 different combinations that you could roll (6*6 = 36). Four of those thirty-six possibilities give you a sum of 9. Four possibilities of rolling a 9 out of thirty-six total possibilities = 4/36 = 1/9. So that means there is a 1/9 chance that would roll a 9, without any restrictions. Once you add restrictions, such as having to roll doubles, then your odds are guaranteed to go down and be less than 1/9. Since the odds have to be less than 1/9, the only answer choice that satisfies that requirement, is choice A, which is zero, making choice A correct.

Sample Question from the Language and Literature Test

Alice Fletcher, the Margaret Mead of her day, assisted several American Indian nations that were threatened with removal from their land to the Indian Territory. She helped them in petitioning Congress for legal titles to their farms. When no response came from Washington, she went there herself to present their case.

According to the statement above, Alice Fletcher attempted to:
- imitate the studies of Margaret Mead
- obtain property rights for American Indians
- protect the integrity of the Indian Territory
- persuade Washington to expand the Indian Territory

Let's look at a couple of different methods of solving this problem.

- Identify the key words in each answer choice. These are the nouns and verbs that are the most important words in the answer choice.
  - imitate, studies
  - obtain, property rights
  - protect, integrity
  - persuade, expand

Now try to match up each of the key words with the passage and see where they fit. You're trying to find synonyms between the key words in the answer choices and key words in the passage.
- imitate – no matches; studies – no matches
- obtain – no matches; property rights – matches with "legal titles" in sentence 2.
- protect – no matches; integrity – no matches
- persuade – matches with "petitioning" in sentence 2; expand – no matches

At this point there are only two choices that have any matches, choice B and D, and they both have matches with sentence 2. This is a good sign, because MCAS will often write two answer choices that are close. Having two answer choices pointing towards sentence 2 as containing the key to the passage (and no other answer choices pointing to any other sentences) is a strong indicator that sentence 2 is the most likely sentence in which to find the answer.

Now let's compare choice B and D and the unmatched key words. Choice B still has "obtain" which doesn't have a clear match, while choice D has "expand" which doesn't have a clear match. To get into the mindset of Alice Fletcher, ask yourself a quick series of questions related to sentence 2.

Sentence 2 states "She helped them in petitioning Congress for legal titles to their farms."

Ask yourself, "Why did she do that?"

Answer: The American Indian nations wanted legal title to their farms and didn't already have it.

Then ask yourself: "So what did Alice Fletcher do?"

Answer: "She tried to help them get the legal title to their farms they wanted."

Now you've suddenly got that match. "Obtain" matches with "get", so your above answer could read, "She tried to help them get (or obtain) the legal title to their farms they wanted."

2. Use a process of elimination.

A. imitate the studies of Margaret Mead – Margaret Mead is only mentioned as a point of historical reference. The passage makes no mention of Mead's studies, only that Alice Fletcher is similar to her.

B. obtain property rights for American Indians – The passage discusses how American Indians were threatened with removal from their land, but Alice Fletcher helped them get legal title, going all the way to Washington to press their case. This is the correct answer. "Obtain property rights for American Indians" is exactly what she fought for.

C. protect the integrity of the Indian Territory – Protecting the integrity of a territory or area deals with maintaining a status quo of a boundary or border. Yet boundaries and borders aren't even mentioned in this passage, only property rights. It wasn't a boundary that Alice Fletcher was fighting to maintain, but rather the right for the American Indians to even live on the land at all.

D. persuade Washington to expand the Indian Territory – At first, this sounds like a good answer choice. Alice Fletcher was trying to persuade Washington. The difference though is that she wasn't trying to persuade them to expand the Indian Territory but legitimize it, i.e. grant legal title. "Expand" suggests dealing with an increase in square mileage, not the ownership at stake – remember the American Indians were threatened with removal from the land, not fighting to increase the amount of land under their control.

Sample Topic for the Composition Test

Possessions can be extremely difficult to give up or lose. Some people believe that is an evolutionary adaptation to cling to assets which are necessary for survival. Others feel that it is due to a personal attachment that develops over the years as emotional memories become linked to inanimate objects.

Your purpose is to write an essay, in which you take a position on whether you believe that attachment to possessions is an evolutionary adaptation for survival or that the attachment stems from a more human element of emotions. Be sure to support your position with logical arguments and appropriate examples.

Let's look at a few different methods and steps to solving this problem.

1. What's the Goal?

Remember that on the essay portion of the MCAS, there isn't a "correct" answer. The response you choose to give to the topic provided does not have to be the first thing that comes to your mind. In fact, the side or response you pick doesn't even have to support the side of the topic that you actually believe in. It is better to have a good explanation for the position, rather than to actually believe in the position on the topic. However, typically you will find that the side you believe in is also the side that you have the most information that you can write about.

To go through some of the steps that you could walk through as you develop your response, let's choose to support the belief that the attachment develops over the years.

As you consider some good examples of possessions, your first thought might be the importance of your home or car, which are necessary for the basic functions of life, such as providing a roof over your head and a method of transportation. Yet, what would be your supporting answer about why your car is important and would be difficult to give up? Some possibilities might be: "it gets me where I need to go, it is brand new, it is expensive, I like it a lot, it would be difficult to replace, it's shiny."

These answer choices may fill up some space, but don't have much meaning. There are other possessions in your life that have much more meaning and priority in other ways that would be better to write about.

Think of possessions that have meaning beyond the mere basics of shelter or transportation. You want a examples that you could potentially write pages and pages about, filling each of them with depths of passionate detail. While you probably won't have time to write pages and pages, it's good to have a examples that have plenty of room to be expanded upon.

2. Make a Short List

The best way to think of examples you would want to include might be to create a short list of possibilities.

What are some that you would truly hate to give up? What are things that you would regret and miss for years to come? What are items that would fit the description of having an emotional attachment develop over the years? Perhaps a precious heirloom, a family antique, or a faded photograph would be suitable examples.

After you've made your list, look back over it and see which possessions you could write the most information about. Those are the ones you would want to include as examples.

3. Answer "Why"

Notice that choosing possessions and writing about them is not the only thing that you have to do. You have to explain your position. You have to answer the "Why."

That is an all-important question. If you wrote a sentence as part of your response and one of the essay scorers looked over your shoulder and said, "but why?" would your next sentence answer their question.

For example, suppose you wrote, "The old chair that used to belong to my grandfather has a lot of meaning."

If someone asked, "But why?" would your next sentence answer it.

Your next sentence should say, "It has meaning because it was the one chair that my grandfather would sit in every day and tell stories from."

Answering the "Why" question is crucial to your success at writing a great essay. It doesn't do any good to write a good essay if it doesn't answer that question.

Sample Question from the Mathematics Test

Table 1

Length of 0.10 mm diameter aluminum wire(m)	Resistance (ohms) at 20° C
1	3.55
2	7.10
4	14.20
10	35.50

Based on the information in Table 1, one would predict that a 20 m length of aluminum wire with a 0.10 mm diameter would have a resistance of:

- 16 ohms

- 25 ohms

- 34 ohms

- 71 ohms

Let's look at a few different methods and steps to solving this problem.

1. Create a Proportion or Ratio

The first way you could approach this problem is by setting up a proportion or ratio. You will find that many of the problems on the MCAS can be solved using this simple technique. Usually whenever you have a given pair of numbers (this number goes with that number) and you are given a third number and asked to find what number would be its match, then you have a problem that can be converted into an easy proportion or ratio.

- 68 -

In this case you can take any of the pairs of numbers from Table 1. As an example, let's choose the second set of numbers (2 m and 7.10 ohms).

Form a question with the information you have at your disposal: 2 meters goes to 7.10 ohms as 20 meters (from the question) goes to which resistance?

From your ratio: 2m/7.10 ohms = 20m/x
"x" is used as the missing number that you will solve for.

Cross multiplication provides us with 2*x = 7.10*20 or 2x = 142.

Dividing both sides by 2 gives us 2x/2 = 142/2 or x = 71, making choice D correct.

2. Use Algebra

The question is asking for the resistance of a 20 m length of wire. The resistance is a function of the length of the wire, so you know that you could probably set up an algebra problem that would have 20 multiplied by some factor "x" that would give you your answer.

So, now you have 20*x = ?

But what exactly is "x"? If 20*x would give you the resistance of a 20 meter piece of wire, than 1*x would give you the resistance of a 1 meter piece of wire. Remember though, the table already told you the resistance of a 1 meter piece of wire – it's 3.55 ohms.

So, if 1*x = 3.55 ohms, then solving for "x" gives you x = 3.55 ohms.

Plugging your solution for "x" back into your initial equation of 20*x = ?, you now have 20*3.55 ohms = 71 ohms, making choice D correct.

3. Look for a Pattern

Much of the time you can get by with just looking for patterns on problems that provide you with a lot of different numbers. In this case, consider the provided table.

1 – 3.55
2 – 7.10
4 – 14.20
10 – 35.50

What patterns do you see in the above number sequences. It appears that when the number in the first column doubled from 1 to 2, the numbers in the second column doubled as well, going from 3.55 to 7.10. Further inspection shows that when the numbers in the first column doubled from 2 to 4, the numbers in the second column doubled again, going from 7.10 to 14.20. Now you've got a pattern, when the first column of numbers doubles, so does the second column.

Since the question asked about a resistance of 20, you should recognize that 20 is the double of 10. Since a length of 10 meant a resistance of 35.50 ohms, then doubling the length of 10 should double the resistance, making 71 ohms, or choice D, correct.

4. Use Logic

A method that works even faster than finding patterns or setting up equations is using simple logic. It appears that as the first number (the length of the wire) gets larger, so does the second number (the resistance).

Since the length of 10 (the largest length wire in the provided table) has a corresponding resistance of 35.50, then another length (such as 20 in the question) should have a length greater than 35.50. As you inspect the answer choices, there is only one answer choice that is greater than 35.50, which is choice D, making it correct.

Mathematics Appendix: Area, Volume, Surface Area Formulas

($\underline{pi}$ = π = 3.141592...)

Areas

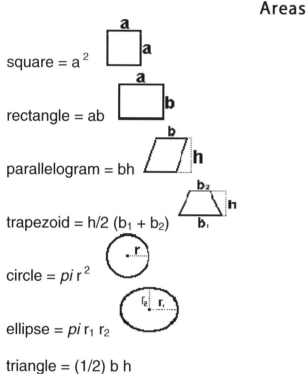

square = a^2

rectangle = ab

parallelogram = bh

trapezoid = h/2 (b_1 + b_2)

circle = $pi\, r^2$

ellipse = $pi\, r_1\, r_2$

triangle = (1/2) b h

Volumes

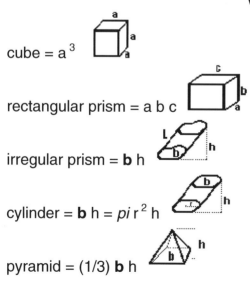

cube = a^3

rectangular prism = a b c

irregular prism = **b** h

cylinder = **b** h = $pi\, r^2$ h

pyramid = (1/3) **b** h

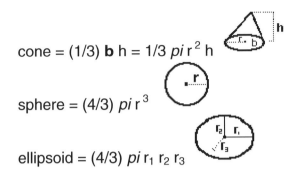

cone = (1/3) **b** h = 1/3 $pi\, r^2$ h

sphere = (4/3) $pi\, r^3$

ellipsoid = (4/3) $pi\, r_1\, r_2\, r_3$

Surface Area

cube = 6 a^2

rectangular prism (3 sides of length a,b,c) = 2*a*b + 2*a*c + 2*b*c

sphere = 4 $pi\, r^2$

Special Report: What Your Test Score Will Tell You About Your IQ

Did you know that most standardized tests correlate very strongly with IQ? In fact, your general intelligence is a better predictor of your success than any other factor, and most tests intentionally measure this trait to some degree to ensure that those selected by the test are truly qualified for the test's purposes.

Before we can delve into the relation between your test score and IQ, I will first have to explain what exactly is IQ. Here's the formula:

Your IQ = 100 + (Number of standard deviations below or above the average)*15

Now, let's define standard deviations by using an example. If we have 5 people with 5 different heights, then first we calculate the average. Let's say the average was 65 inches. The standard deviation is the "average distance" away from the average of each of the members. It is a direct measure of variability - if the 5 people included Jackie Chan and Shaquille O'Neal, obviously there's a lot more variability in that group than a group of 5 sisters who are all within 6 inches in height of each other. The standard deviation uses a number to characterize the average range of difference within a group.

A convenient feature of most groups is that they have a "normal" distribution-makes sense that most things would be normal, right? Without getting into a bunch of statistical mumbo-jumbo, you just need to know that if you know the average of the group and the standard deviation, you can successfully predict someone's percentile rank in the group.

Confused? Let me give you an example. If instead of 5 people's heights, we had 100 people, we could figure out their rank in height JUST by knowing the average, standard deviation, and their height. We wouldn't need to know each person's height and manually rank them, we could just predict their rank based on three numbers.

What this means is that you can take your PERCENTILE rank that is often given with your test and relate this to your RELATIVE IQ of people taking the test - that is, your IQ relative to the people taking the test. Obviously, there's no way to know your actual IQ because the people taking a standardized test are usually not very good samples of the general population- many of those with extremely low IQ's never achieve a level of success or competency necessary to complete a typical standardized test. In fact, professional psychologists who measure IQ actually have to use non-written tests that can fairly measure the IQ of those not able to complete a traditional test.

The bottom line is to not take your test score too seriously, but it is fun to compute your "relative IQ" among the people who took the test with you. I've done the calculations below. Just look up your percentile rank in the left and then you'll see your "relative IQ" for your test in the right hand column-

Percentile Rank	Your Relative IQ		Percentile Rank	Your Relative IQ
99	135		59	103
98	131		58	103
97	128		57	103
96	126		56	102
95	125		55	102
94	123		54	102
93	122		53	101
92	121		52	101
91	120		51	100
90	119		50	100
89	118		49	100
88	118		48	99
87	117		47	99
86	116		46	98
85	116		45	98

84	115	44	98
83	114	43	97
82	114	42	97
81	113	41	97
80	113	40	96
79	112	39	96
78	112	38	95
77	111	37	95
76	111	36	95
75	110	35	94
74	110	34	94
73	109	33	93
72	109	32	93
71	108	31	93
70	108	30	92
69	107	29	92
68	107	28	91
67	107	27	91
66	106	26	90
65	106	25	90
64	105	24	89
63	105	23	89
62	105	22	88
61	104	21	88
60	104	20	87

Special Report: Retaking the Test: What Are Your Chances at Improving Your Score?

After going through the experience of taking a major test, many test takers feel that once is enough. The test usually comes during a period of transition in the test taker's life, and taking the test is only one of a series of important events. With so many distractions and conflicting recommendations, it may be difficult for a test taker to rationally determine whether or not he should retake the test after viewing his scores.

The importance of the test usually only adds to the burden of the retake decision. However, don't be swayed by emotion. There a few simple questions that you can ask yourself to guide you as you try to determine whether a retake would improve your score:

1. What went wrong? Why wasn't your score what you expected?

Can you point to a single factor or problem that you feel caused the low score? Were you sick on test day? Was there an emotional upheaval in your life that caused a distraction? Were you late for the test or not able to use the full time allotment? If you can point to any of these specific, individual problems, then a retake should definitely be considered.

2. Is there enough time to improve?

Many problems that may show up in your score report may take a lot of time for improvement. A deficiency in a particular math skill may require weeks or months of tutoring and studying to improve. If you have enough time to improve an identified weakness, then a retake should definitely be considered.

3. How will additional scores be used? Will a score average, highest score, or most recent score be used?

Different test scores may be handled completely differently. If you've taken the test multiple times, sometimes your highest score is used, sometimes your average score is computed and used, and sometimes your most recent score is used. Make sure you understand what method will be used to evaluate your scores, and use that to help you determine whether a retake should be considered.

4. Are my practice test scores significantly higher than my actual test score?

If you have taken a lot of practice tests and are consistently scoring at a much higher level than your actual test score, then you should consider a retake. However, if you've taken five practice tests and only one of your scores was higher than your actual test score, or if your practice test scores were only slightly higher than your actual test score, then it is unlikely that you will significantly increase your score.

5. Do I need perfect scores or will I be able to live with this score? Will this score still allow me to follow my dreams?

What kind of score is acceptable to you? Is your current score "good enough?" Do you have to have a certain score in order to pursue the future of your dreams? If you won't be happy with your current score, and there's no way that you could live with it, then you should consider a retake. However, don't get your hopes up. If you are looking for significant improvement, that may or may not be possible. But if you won't be happy otherwise, it is at least worth the effort.

Remember that there are other considerations. To achieve your dream, it is likely that your grades may also be taken into account. A great test score is usually not the only thing necessary to succeed. Make sure that you aren't overemphasizing the importance of a high test score.

Furthermore, a retake does not always result in a higher score. Some test takers will score lower on a retake, rather than higher. One study shows that one-fourth of test takers will achieve a significant improvement in test score, while one-sixth of test takers will actually show a decrease. While this shows that most test takers will improve, the majority will only improve their scores a little and a retake may not be worth the test taker's effort.

Finally, if a test is taken only once and is considered in the added context of good grades on the part of a test taker, the person reviewing the grades and scores may be tempted to assume that the test taker just had a bad day while taking the test, and may discount the low test score in favor of the high grades. But if the test is retaken and the scores are approximately the same, then the validity of the low scores are only confirmed. Therefore, a retake could actually hurt a test taker by definitely bracketing a test taker's score ability to a limited range.

Special Report: What is Test Anxiety and How to Overcome It?

The very nature of tests caters to some level of anxiety, nervousness or tension, just as we feel for any important event that occurs in our lives. A little bit of anxiety or nervousness can be a good thing. It helps us with motivation, and makes achievement just that much sweeter. However, too much anxiety can be a problem; especially if it hinders our ability to function and perform.

"Test anxiety," is the term that refers to the emotional reactions that some test-takers experience when faced with a test or exam. Having a fear of testing and exams is based upon a rational fear, since the test-taker's performance can shape the course of an academic career. Nevertheless, experiencing excessive fear of examinations will only interfere with the test-takers ability to perform, and his/her chances to be successful.

There are a large variety of causes that can contribute to the development and sensation of test anxiety. These include, but are not limited to lack of performance and worrying about issues surrounding the test.

Lack of Preparation

Lack of preparation can be identified by the following behaviors or situations:

Not scheduling enough time to study, and therefore cramming the night before the test or exam

Managing time poorly, to create the sensation that there is not enough time to do everything

Failing to organize the text information in advance, so that the study material consists of the entire text and not simply the pertinent information

Poor overall studying habits

Worrying, on the other hand, can be related to both the test taker, or many other factors around him/her that will be affected by the results of the test. These include worrying about:

Previous performances on similar exams, or exams in general

How friends and other students are achieving

The negative consequences that will result from a poor grade or failure

There are three primary elements to test anxiety. Physical components, which involve the same typical bodily reactions as those to acute anxiety (to be discussed below). Emotional factors have to do with fear or panic. Mental or cognitive issues concerning attention spans and memory abilities.

Physical Signals

There are many different symptoms of test anxiety, and these are not limited to mental and emotional strain. Frequently there are a range of physical signals that will let a test taker know that he/she is suffering from test anxiety. These bodily changes can include the following:

Perspiring

Sweaty palms

Wet, trembling hands

Nausea

Dry mouth

A knot in the stomach

Headache

Faintness

Muscle tension

Aching shoulders, back and neck

Rapid heart beat

Feeling too hot/cold

To recognize the sensation of test anxiety, a test-taker should monitor him/herself for the following sensations:

The physical distress symptoms as listed above

Emotional sensitivity, expressing emotional feelings such as the need to cry or laugh too much, or a sensation of anger or helplessness

A decreased ability to think, causing the test-taker to blank out or have racing thoughts that are hard to organize or control.

Though most students will feel some level of anxiety when faced with a test or exam, the majority can cope with that anxiety and maintain it at a manageable level. However, those who cannot are faced with a very real and very serious condition, which can and should be controlled for the immeasurable benefit of this sufferer.

Naturally, these sensations lead to negative results for the testing experience. The most common effects of test anxiety have to do with nervousness and mental blocking.

Nervousness

Nervousness can appear in several different levels:

The test-taker's difficulty, or even inability to read and understand the questions on the test

The difficulty or inability to organize thoughts to a coherent form

The difficulty or inability to recall key words and concepts relating to the testing questions (especially essays)

The receipt of poor grades on a test, though the test material was well known by the test taker

Conversely, a person may also experience mental blocking, which involves:

Blanking out on test questions

Only remembering the correct answers to the questions when the test has already finished.

Fortunately for test anxiety sufferers, beating these feelings, to a large degree, has to do with proper preparation. When a test taker has a feeling of preparedness, then anxiety will be dramatically lessened.

The first step to resolving anxiety issues is to distinguish which of the two types of anxiety are being suffered. If the anxiety is a direct result of a lack of preparation, this should be considered a normal reaction, and the anxiety level (as opposed to the test results) shouldn't be anything to worry about. However, if, when adequately prepared, the test-taker still panics, blanks out, or seems to overreact, this is not a fully rational reaction. While this can be considered normal too, there are many ways to combat and overcome these effects.

Remember that anxiety cannot be entirely eliminated, however, there are ways to minimize it, to make the anxiety easier to manage. Preparation is one of the best ways to minimize test anxiety. Therefore the following techniques are wise in order to best fight off any anxiety that may want to build.

To begin with, try to avoid cramming before a test, whenever it is possible. By trying to memorize an entire term's worth of information in one day, you'll be shocking your system, and not giving yourself a very good chance to absorb the information. This is an easy path to anxiety, so for those who suffer from test anxiety, cramming should not even be considered an option.

Instead of cramming, work throughout the semester to combine all of the material which is presented throughout the semester, and work on it gradually as the course goes by, making sure to master the main concepts first, leaving minor details for a week or so before the test.

To study for the upcoming exam, be sure to pose questions that may be on the examination, to gauge the ability to answer them by integrating the ideas from your texts, notes and lectures, as well as any supplementary readings.

If it is truly impossible to cover all of the information that was covered in that particular term, concentrate on the most important portions, that can be covered very well. Learn these concepts as best as possible, so that when the test comes, a goal can be made to use these concepts as presentations of your knowledge.

In addition to study habits, changes in attitude are critical to beating a struggle with test anxiety. In fact, an improvement of the perspective over the entire test-taking experience can actually help a test taker to enjoy studying and therefore improve the overall experience. Be certain not to overemphasize the significance of the grade - know that the result of the test is neither a reflection of self worth, nor is it a measure of intelligence; one grade will not predict a person's future success.

To improve an overall testing outlook, the following steps should be tried:

- Keeping in mind that the most reasonable expectation for taking a test is to expect to try to demonstrate as much of what you know as you possibly can.

- Reminding ourselves that a test is only one test; this is not the only one, and there will be others.

- The thought of thinking of oneself in an irrational, all-or-nothing term should be avoided at all costs.

- A reward should be designated for after the test, so there's something to look forward to. Whether it be going to a movie, going out to eat, or simply visiting friends, schedule it in advance, and do it no matter what result is expected on the exam.

Test-takers should also keep in mind that the basics are some of the most important things, even beyond anti-anxiety techniques and studying. Never neglect the basic social, emotional and biological needs, in order to try to absorb information. In order to best achieve, these three factors must be held as just as important as the studying itself.

Study Steps

Remember the following important steps for studying:

- Maintain healthy nutrition and exercise habits. Continue both your recreational activities and social pass times. These both contribute to your physical and emotional well being.

- Be certain to get a good amount of sleep, especially the night before the test, because when you're overtired you are not able to perform to the best of your best ability.

- Keep the studying pace to a moderate level by taking breaks when they are needed, and varying the work whenever possible, to keep the mind fresh instead of getting bored.

- When enough studying has been done that all the material that can be learned has been learned, and the test taker is prepared for the test, stop studying and do something relaxing such as listening to music, watching a movie, or taking a warm bubble bath.

There are also many other techniques to minimize the uneasiness or apprehension that is experienced along with test anxiety before, during, or even after the examination. In fact, there are a great deal of things that can be done to stop anxiety from interfering with lifestyle and performance. Again, remember that anxiety will not be eliminated entirely, and it shouldn't be. Otherwise that "up" feeling for exams would not exist, and most of us depend on that sensation to perform better than usual. However, this anxiety has to be at a level that is manageable.

Of course, as we have just discussed, being prepared for the exam is half the battle right away. Attending all classes, finding out what knowledge will be expected on the exam, and knowing the exam schedules are easy steps to lowering anxiety. Keeping up with work will remove the need to cram, and efficient study habits will eliminate wasted time. Studying should be done in an ideal location for concentration, so that it is simple to become interested in the material and give it complete attention. A method such as SQ3R (Survey, Question, Read, Recite, Review) is a wonderful key to follow to make sure that the study habits are as effective as possible, especially in the case of learning from a textbook. Flashcards are great techniques for memorization. Learning to take good notes will mean that notes will be full of useful information, so that less sifting will need to be done to seek out what is pertinent for studying. Reviewing notes after class and then again on occasion will keep the information fresh in the mind. From notes that have been taken summary sheets and outlines can be made for simpler reviewing.

A study group can also be a very motivational and helpful place to study, as there will be a sharing of ideas, all of the minds can work together, to make sure that everyone understands, and the studying will be made more interesting because it will be a social occasion.

Basically, though, as long as the test-taker remains organized and self confident, with efficient study habits, less time will need to be spent studying, and higher grades will be achieved.

To become self confident, there are many useful steps. The first of these is "self talk." It has been shown through extensive research, that self-talk for students who suffer from test anxiety, should be well monitored, in order to make sure that it contributes to self confidence as opposed to sinking the student. Frequently the self talk of test-anxious students is negative or self-defeating, thinking that everyone else is smarter and faster, that they always mess up, and that if they don't do well, they'll fail the entire course. It is important to decreasing anxiety that awareness is made of self talk. Try writing any negative self thoughts and then disputing them with a positive statement instead. Begin self-encouragement as though it was a friend speaking. Repeat positive statements to help reprogram the mind to believing in successes instead of failures.

Helpful Techniques

Other extremely helpful techniques include:

- Self-visualization of doing well and reaching goals
- While aiming for an "A" level of understanding, don't try to "overprotect" by setting your expectations lower. This will only convince the mind to stop studying in order to meet the lower expectations.

- Don't make comparisons with the results or habits of other students. These are individual factors, and different things work for different people, causing different results.

- Strive to become an expert in learning what works well, and what can be done in order to improve. Consider collecting this data in a journal.

- Create rewards for after studying instead of doing things before studying that will only turn into avoidance behaviors.

- Make a practice of relaxing - by using methods such as progressive relaxation, self-hypnosis, guided imagery, etc - in order to make relaxation an automatic sensation.

- Work on creating a state of relaxed concentration so that concentrating will take on the focus of the mind, so that none will be wasted on worrying.

- Take good care of the physical self by eating well and getting enough sleep.

- Plan in time for exercise and stick to this plan.

Beyond these techniques, there are other methods to be used before, during and after the test that will help the test-taker perform well in addition to overcoming anxiety.

Before the exam comes the academic preparation. This involves establishing a study schedule and beginning at least one week before the actual date of the test. By doing this, the anxiety of not having enough time to study for the test will be automatically eliminated. Moreover, this will make the studying a much more effective experience, ensuring that the learning will be an easier process. This relieves much undue pressure on the test-taker.

Summary sheets, note cards, and flash cards with the main concepts and examples of these main concepts should be prepared in advance of the actual studying time. A topic should never be eliminated from this process. By omitting a topic because it isn't expected to be on the test is only setting up the test-taker for anxiety should it actually appear on the exam. Utilize the course syllabus for laying out the topics that should be studied. Carefully go over the notes that were made in class, paying special attention to any of the issues that the professor took special care to emphasize while lecturing in class. In the textbooks, use the chapter review, or if possible, the chapter tests, to begin your review.

It may even be possible to ask the instructor what information will be covered on the exam, or what the format of the exam will be (for example, multiple choice, essay, free form, true-false). Additionally, see if it is possible to find out how many questions will be on the test. If a review sheet or sample test has been offered by the professor, make good use of it, above anything else, for the preparation for the test. Another great resource for getting to know the examination is reviewing tests from previous semesters. Use these tests to review, and aim to achieve a 100% score on each of the possible topics. With a few exceptions, the goal that you set for yourself is the highest one that you will reach.

Take all of the questions that were assigned as homework, and rework them to any other possible course material. The more problems reworked, the more skill and confidence will form as a result. When forming the solution to a problem, write out each of the steps. Don't simply do head work. By doing as many steps on paper as possible, much clarification and therefore confidence will be formed. Do this with as many homework problems as possible, before checking the answers. By checking the answer after each problem, a reinforcement will exist, that will not be on the exam. Study situations should be as exam-like as possible, to prime the test-taker's system for the experience. By waiting to check the answers at the end, a psychological advantage will be formed, to decrease the stress factor.

Another fantastic reason for not cramming is the avoidance of confusion in concepts, especially when it comes to mathematics. 8-10 hours of study will become one hundred percent more effective if it is spread out over a week or at least several days, instead of doing it all in one sitting. Recognize that the human brain requires time in order to assimilate new material, so frequent breaks and a span of study time over several days will be much more beneficial.

Additionally, don't study right up until the point of the exam. Studying should stop a minimum of one hour before the exam begins. This allows the brain to rest and put things in their proper order. This will also provide the time to become as relaxed as possible when going into the examination room. The test-taker will also have time to eat well and eat sensibly. Know that the brain needs food as much as the rest of the body. With enough food and enough sleep, as well as a relaxed attitude, the body and the mind are primed for success.

Avoid any anxious classmates who are talking about the exam. These students only spread anxiety, and are not worth sharing the anxious sentimentalities.

Before the test also involves creating a positive attitude, so mental preparation should also be a point of concentration. There are many keys to creating a positive attitude. Should fears become rushing in, make a visualization of taking the exam, doing well, and seeing an A written on the paper. Write out a list of affirmations that will bring a feeling of confidence, such as "I am doing well in my English class," "I studied well and know my material," "I enjoy this class." Even if the affirmations aren't believed at first, it sends a positive message to the subconscious which will result in an alteration of the overall belief system, which is the system that creates reality.

If a sensation of panic begins, work with the fear and imagine the very worst! Work through the entire scenario of not passing the test, failing the entire course, and dropping out of school, followed by not getting a job, and pushing a shopping cart through the dark alley where you'll live. This will place things into perspective! Then, practice deep breathing and create a visualization of the opposite situation - achieving an "A" on the exam, passing the entire course, receiving the degree at a graduation ceremony.

On the day of the test, there are many things to be done to ensure the best results, as well as the most calm outlook. The following stages are suggested in order to maximize test-taking potential:

- Begin the examination day with a moderate breakfast, and avoid any coffee or beverages with caffeine if the test taker is prone to jitters. Even people who are used to managing caffeine can feel jittery or light-headed when it is taken on a test day.
- Attempt to do something that is relaxing before the examination begins. As last minute cramming clouds the mastering of overall concepts, it is better to use this time to create a calming outlook.
- Be certain to arrive at the test location well in advance, in order to provide time to select a location that is away from doors, windows and other distractions, as well as giving enough time to relax before the test begins.
- Keep away from anxiety generating classmates who will upset the sensation of stability and relaxation that is being attempted before the exam.
- Should the waiting period before the exam begins cause anxiety, create a self-distraction by reading a light magazine or something else that is relaxing and simple.

During the exam itself, read the entire exam from beginning to end, and find out how much time should be allotted to each individual problem. Once writing the exam, should more time be taken for a problem, it should be abandoned, in order to begin another problem. If there is time at the end, the unfinished problem can always be returned to and completed.

Read the instructions very carefully - twice - so that unpleasant surprises won't follow during or after the exam has ended.

When writing the exam, pretend that the situation is actually simply the completion of homework within a library, or at home. This will assist in forming a relaxed atmosphere, and will allow the brain extra focus for the complex thinking function.

Begin the exam with all of the questions with which the most confidence is felt. This will build the confidence level regarding the entire exam and will begin a quality momentum. This will also create encouragement for trying the problems where uncertainty resides.

Going with the "gut instinct" is always the way to go when solving a problem. Second guessing should be avoided at all costs. Have confidence in the ability to do well.

For essay questions, create an outline in advance that will keep the mind organized and make certain that all of the points are remembered. For multiple choice, read every answer, even if the correct one has been spotted - a better one may exist.

Continue at a pace that is reasonable and not rushed, in order to be able to work carefully. Provide enough time to go over the answers at the end, to check for small errors that can be corrected.

Should a feeling of panic begin, breathe deeply, and think of the feeling of the body releasing sand through its pores. Visualize a calm, peaceful place, and include all of the sights, sounds and sensations of this image. Continue the deep breathing, and take a few minutes to continue this with closed eyes. When all is well again, return to the test.

If a "blanking" occurs for a certain question, skip it and move on to the next question. There will be time to return to the other question later. Get everything done that can be done, first, to guarantee all the grades that can be compiled, and to build all of the confidence possible. Then return to the weaker questions to build the marks from there.

Remember, one's own reality can be created, so as long as the belief is there, success will follow. And remember: anxiety can happen later, right now, there's an exam to be written!

After the examination is complete, whether there is a feeling for a good grade or a bad grade, don't dwell on the exam, and be certain to follow through on the reward that was promised…and enjoy it! Don't dwell on any mistakes that have been made, as there is nothing that can be done at this point anyway.

Additionally, don't begin to study for the next test right away. Do something relaxing for a while, and let the mind relax and prepare itself to begin absorbing information again.

From the results of the exam - both the grade and the entire experience, be certain to learn from what has gone on. Perfect studying habits and work some more on confidence in order to make the next examination experience even better than the last one.

Learn to avoid places where openings occurred for laziness, procrastination and day dreaming.

Use the time between this exam and the next one to better learn to relax, even learning to relax on cue, so that any anxiety can be controlled during the next exam. Learn how to relax the body. Slouch in your chair if that helps. Tighten and then relax all of the different muscle groups, one group at a time, beginning with the feet and then working all the way up to the neck and face. This will ultimately relax the muscles more than they were to begin with. Learn how to breathe deeply and comfortably, and focus on this breathing going in and out as a relaxing thought. With every exhale, repeat the word "relax."

As common as test anxiety is, it is very possible to overcome it. Make yourself one of the test-takers who overcome this frustrating hindrance.

Special Report: How to Overcome Your Fear of Math

If this article started by saying "Math," many of us would feel a shiver crawl up our spines, just by reading that simple word. Images of torturous years in those crippling desks of the math classes can become so vivid to our consciousness that we can almost smell those musty textbooks, and see the smudges of the #2 pencils on our fingers.

If you are still a student, feeling the impact of these sometimes overwhelming classroom sensations, you are not alone if you get anxious at just the thought of taking that compulsory math course. Does your heart beat just that much faster when you have to split the bill for lunch among your friends with a group of your friends? Do you truly believe that you simply don't have the brain for math? Certainly you're good at other things, but math just simply isn't one of them? Have you ever avoided activities, or other school courses because they appear to involve mathematics, with which you're simply not comfortable?

If any one or more of these "symptoms" can be applied to you, you could very well be suffering from a very real condition called "Math Anxiety."

It's not at all uncommon for people to think that they have some sort of math disability or allergy, when in actuality, their block is a direct result of the way in which they were taught math!

In the late 1950's with the dawning of the space age, New Math - a new "fuzzy math" reform that focuses on higher-order thinking, conceptual understanding and solving problems - took the country by storm. It's now becoming ever more clear that teachers were not supplied with the correct, practical and effective way in which they should be teaching new math so that students will understand the methods comfortably. So is it any wonder that so many students struggled so deeply, when their teachers were required to change their entire math systems without the foundation of proper training? Even if you have not been personally, directly affected by that precise event, its impact is still as rampant as ever.

Basically, the math teachers of today are either the teachers who began teaching the new math in the first place (without proper training) or they are the students of the math teachers who taught new math without proper training. Therefore, unless they had a unique, exceptional teacher, their primary, consistent examples of teaching math have been teachers using methods that are not conducive to the general understanding of the entire class. This explains why your discomfort (or fear) of math is not at all rare.

It is very clear why being called up to the chalk board to solve a math problem is such a common example of a terrifying situation for students - and it has very little to do with a fear of being in front of the class. Most of us have had a minimum of one humiliating experience while standing with chalk dusted fingers, with the eyes of every math student piercing through us. These are the images that haunt us all the way through adulthood. But it does not mean that we cannot learn math. It just means that we could be developing a solid case of math anxiety.

But what exactly is math anxiety? It's an very strong emotional sensation of anxiety, panic, or fear that people feel when they think about or must apply their ability to understand mathematics. Sufferers of math anxiety frequently believe that they are incapable of doing activities or taking classes that involve math skills. In fact, some people with math anxiety have developed such a fear that it has become a phobia; aptly named math phobia.

The incidence of math anxiety, especially among college students, but also among high school students, has risen considerably over the last 10 years, and currently this increase shows no signs of slowing down. Frequently students will even chose their college majors and programs based specifically on how little math will be compulsory for the completion of the degree.

The prevalence of math anxiety has become so dramatic on college campuses that many of these schools have special counseling programs that are designed to assist math anxious students to deal with their discomfort and their math problems.

Math anxiety itself is not an intellectual problem, as many people have been lead to believe; it is, in fact, an emotional problem that stems from improper math teaching techniques that have slowly built and reinforced these feelings. However, math anxiety can result in an intellectual problem when its symptoms interfere with a person's ability to learn and understand math.

The fear of math can cause a sort of "glitch" in the brain that can cause an otherwise clever person to stumble over even the simplest of math problems. A study by Dr. Mark H. Ashcraft of Cleveland State University in Ohio showed that college students who usually perform well, but who suffer from math anxiety, will suffer from fleeting lapses in their working memory when they are asked to perform even the most basic mental arithmetic. These same issues regarding memory were not present in the same students when they were required to answer questions that did not involve numbers. This very clearly demonstrated that the memory phenomenon is quite specific to only math.

So what exactly is it that causes this inhibiting math anxiety? Unfortunately it is not as simple as one answer, since math anxiety doesn't have one specific cause.

Frequently math anxiety can result of a student's either negative experience or embarrassment with math or a math teacher in previous years.

These circumstances can prompt the student to believe that he or she is somehow deficient in his or her math abilities. This belief will consistently lead to a poor performance in math tests and courses in general, leading only to confirm the beliefs of the student's inability. This particular phenomenon is referred to as the "self-fulfilling prophecy" by the psychological community. Math anxiety will result in poor performance, rather than it being the other way around.

Dr. Ashcraft stated that math anxiety is a "It's a learned, almost phobic, reaction to math," and that it is not only people prone to anxiety, fear, or panic who can develop math anxiety. The image alone of doing math problems can send the blood pressure and heart rate to race, even in the calmest person.

The study by Dr. Ashcraft and his colleague Elizabeth P. Kirk, discovered that students who suffered from math anxiety were frequently stumped by issues of even the most basic math rules, such as "carrying over" a number, when performing a sum, or "borrowing" from a number when doing a subtraction. Lapses such as this occurred only on working memory questions involving numbers.

To explain the problem with memory, Ashcraft states that when math anxiety begins to take its effect, the sufferer experiences a rush of thoughts, leaving little room for the focus required to perform even the simplest of math problems. He stated that "you're draining away the energy you need for solving the problem by worrying about it."

The outcome is a "vicious cycle," for students who are sufferers of math anxiety. As math anxiety is developed, the fear it promotes stands in the way of learning, leading to a decrease in self-confidence in the ability to perform even simple arithmetic.

A large portion of the problem lies in the ways in which math is taught to students today. In the US, students are frequently taught the rules of math, but rarely will they learn why a specific approach to a math problems work. Should students be provided with a foundation of "deeper understanding" of math, it may prevent the development of phobias.

Another study that was published in the Journal of Experimental Psychology by Dr. Jamie Campbell and Dr. Qilin Xue of the University of Saskatchewan in Saskatoon, Canada, reflected the same concepts. The researchers in this study looked at university students who were educated in Canada and China, discovering that the Chinese students could generally outperform the Canadian-educated students when it came to solving complex math problems involving procedural knowledge - the ability to know how to solve a math problem, instead of simply having ideas memorized.

A portion of this result seemed to be due to the use of calculators within both elementary and secondary schools; while Canadians frequently used them, the Chinese students did not.

However, calculators were not the only issue. Since Chinese-educated students also outperformed Canadian-educated students in complex math, it is suggested that cultural factors may also have an impact. However, the short-cut of using the calculator may hinder the development of the problem solving skills that are key to performing well in math.

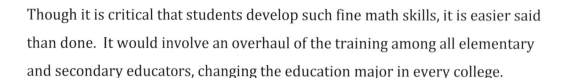

Though it is critical that students develop such fine math skills, it is easier said than done. It would involve an overhaul of the training among all elementary and secondary educators, changing the education major in every college.

Math Myths

One problem that contributes to the progression of math anxiety, is the belief of many math myths. These erroneous math beliefs include the following:

Men are better in math than women - however, research has failed to demonstrate that there is any difference in math ability between the sexes. There is a single best way to solve a math problem - however, the majority of math problems can be solved in a number of different ways. By saying that there is only one way to solve a math problem, the thinking and creative skills of the student are held back.

Some people have a math mind, and others do not - in truth, the majority of people have much more potential for their math capabilities than they believe of themselves.

It is a bad thing to count by using your fingers - counting by using fingers has actually shown that an understanding of arithmetic has been established.

People who are skilled in math can do problems quickly in their heads - in actuality, even math professors will review their example problems before they teach them in their classes.

The anxieties formed by these myths can frequently be perpetuated by a range of mind games that students seem to play with themselves. These math mind games include the following beliefs:

I don't perform math fast enough - actually everyone has a different rate at which he or she can learn. The speed of the solving of math problems is not important as long as the student can solve it.

I don't have the mind for math - this belief can inhibit a student's belief in him or herself, and will therefore interfere with the student's real ability to learn math.

I got the correct answer, but it was done the wrong way - there is no single best way to complete a math problem. By believing this, a student's creativity and overall understanding of math is hindered.

If I can get the correct answer, then it is too simple - students who suffer from math anxiety frequently belittle their own abilities when it comes to their math capabilities.

Math is unrelated to my "real" life - by freeing themselves of the fear of math, math anxiety sufferers are only limiting their choices and freedoms for the rest of their life.

Fortunately, there are many ways to help those who suffer from math anxiety. Since math anxiety is a learned, psychological response to doing or thinking about math, that interferes with the sufferer's ability to understand and perform math, it is not at all a reflection of the sufferer's true math sills and abilities.

Helpful Strategies

Many strategies and therapies have been developed to help students to overcome their math anxious responses. Some of these helpful strategies include the following:

Reviewing and learning basic arithmetic principles, techniques and methods. Frequently math anxiety is a result of the experience of many students with early negative situations, and these students have never truly developed a strong base in basic arithmetic, especially in the case of multiplication and fractions. Since math is a discipline that is built on an accumulative foundation, where the concepts are built upon gradually from simpler concepts, a student who has not achieved a solid basis in arithmetic will experience difficulty in learning higher order math. Taking a remedial math course, or a short math course that focuses on arithmetic can often make a considerable difference in reducing the anxious response that math anxiety sufferers have with math.

Becoming aware of any thoughts, actions and feelings that are related to math and responses to math. Math anxiety has a different effect on different students. Therefore it is very important to become familiar with any reactions that the math anxiety sufferer may have about him/herself and the situation when math has been encountered. If the sufferer becomes aware of any irrational or unrealistic thoughts, it's possible to better concentrate on replacing these thoughts with more positive and realistic ones.

Find help! Math anxiety, as we've mentioned, is a learned response, that is reinforced repeatedly over a period of time, and is therefore not something that can be eliminated instantaneously. Students can more effectively reduce their anxious responses with the help of many different services that are readily available. Seeking the assistance of a psychologist or counselor, especially one with a specialty in math anxiety, can assist the sufferer in performing an analysis of his/her psychological response to math, as well as learning anxiety management skills, and developing effective coping strategies. Other great tools are tutors, classes that teach better abilities to take better notes in math class, and other math learning aids.

Learning the mathematic vocabulary will instantly provide a better chance for understanding new concepts. One major issue among students is the lack of understanding of the terms and vocabulary that are common jargon within math classes. Typically math classes will utilize words in a completely different way from the way in which they are utilized in all other subjects. Students easily mistake their lack of understanding the math terms with their mathematical abilities.

Learning anxiety reducing techniques and methods for anxiety management. Anxiety greatly interferes with a student's ability to concentrate, think clearly, pay attention, and remember new concepts. When these same students can learn to relax, using anxiety management techniques, the student can regain his or her ability to control his or her emotional and physical symptoms of anxiety that interfere with the capabilities of mental processing.

Working on creating a positive overall attitude about mathematics. Looking at math with a positive attitude will reduce anxiety through the building of a positive attitude.

Learning to self-talk in a positive way. Pep talking oneself through a positive self talk can greatly assist in overcoming beliefs in math myths or the mind games that may be played. Positive self-talking is an effective way to replace the negative thoughts - the ones that create the anxiety. Even if the sufferer doesn't believe the statements at first, it plants a positive seed in the subconscious, and allows a positive outlook to grow.

Beyond this, students should learn effective math class, note taking and studying techniques. Typically, the math anxious students will avoid asking questions to save themselves from embarrassment. They will sit in the back of classrooms, and refrain from seeking assistance from the professor. Moreover, they will put off studying for math until the very last moment, since it causes them such substantial discomfort. Alone, or a combination of these negative behaviors work only to reduce the anxiety of the students, but in reality, they are actually building a substantially more intense anxiety.

There are many different positive behaviors that can be adopted by math anxious students, so that they can learn to better perform within their math classes.

Sit near the front of the class. This way, there will be fewer distractions, and there will be more of a sensation of being a part of the topic of discussion.

If any questions arise, ASK! If one student has a question, then there are certain to be others who have the same question but are too nervous to ask - perhaps because they have not yet learned how to deal with their own math anxiety.

Seek extra help from the professor after class or during office hours.

Prepare, prepare, prepare - read textbook material before the class, do the homework and work out any problems available within the textbook. Math skills are developed through practice and repetition, so the more practice and repetition, the better the math skills.

Review the material once again after class, to repeat it another time, and to reinforce the new concepts that were learned.

Beyond these tactics that can be taken by the students themselves, teachers and parents need to know that they can also have a large impact on the reduction of math anxiety within students.

As parents and teachers, there is a natural desire to help students to learn and understand how they will one day utilize different math techniques within their everyday lives. But when the student or teacher displays the symptoms of a person who has had nightmarish memories regarding math, where hesitations then develop in the instruction of students, these fears are automatically picked up by the students and commonly adopted as their own.

However, it is possible for teachers and parents to move beyond their own fears to better educate students by overcoming their own hesitations and learning to enjoy math.

Begin by adopting the outlook that math is a beautiful, imaginative or living thing. Of course, we normally think of mathematics as numbers that can be added or subtracted, multiplied or divided, but that is simply the beginning of it.

By thinking of math as something fun and imaginative, parents and teachers can teach children different ways to manipulate numbers, for example in balancing a checkbook. Parents rarely tell their children that math is everywhere around us; in nature, art, and even architecture. Usually, this is because they were never shown these relatively simple connections. But that pattern can break very simply through the participation of parents and teachers.

The beauty and hidden wonders of mathematics can easily be emphasized through a focus that can open the eyes of students to the incredible mathematical patterns that arise everywhere within the natural world. Observations and discussions can be made into things as fascinating as spider webs, leaf patterns, sunflowers and even coastlines. This makes math not only beautiful, but also inspiring and (dare we say) fun!

Pappas Method

For parents and teachers to assist their students in discovering the true wonders of mathematics, the techniques of Theoni Pappas can easily be applied, as per her popular and celebrated book "Fractals, Googols and Other Mathematical Tales." Pappas used to be a math phobia sufferer and created a fascinating step-by-step program for parents and teachers to use in order to teach students the joy of math.

Her simple, constructive step-by-step program goes as follows:

Don't let your fear of math come across to your kids - Parents must be careful not to perpetuate the mathematical myth - that math is only for specially talented "math types." Strive not to make comments like; "they don't like math" or "I have never been good at math." When children overhear comments like these from their primary role models they begin to dread math before even considering a chance of experiencing its wonders. It is important to encourage your children to read and explore the rich world of mathematics, and to practice mathematics without imparting negative biases.

Don't immediately associate math with computation (counting) - It is very important to realize that math is not just numbers and computations, but a realm of exciting ideas that touch every part of our lives -from making a telephone call to how the hair grows on someone's head. Take your children outside and point out real objects that display math concepts. For example, show them the symmetry of a leaf or angles on a building. Take a close look at the spirals in a spider web or intricate patterns of a snowflake.

Help your child understand why math is important - Math improves problem solving, increases competency and should be applied in different ways. It's the same as reading. You can learn the basics of reading without ever enjoying a novel. But, where's the excitement in that? With math, you could stop with the basics. But why when there is so much more to be gained by a fuller Understanding? Life is so much more enriching when we go beyond the basics. Stretch your children's minds to become involved in mathematics in ways that will not only be practical but also enhance their lives.

Make math as "hands on" as possible - Mathematicians participate in mathematics. To really experience math encourage your child to dig in and tackle problems in creative ways. Help them learn how to manipulate numbers using concrete references they understand as well as things they can see or touch. Look for patterns everywhere, explore shapes and symmetries. How many octagons do you see each day on the way to the grocery store? Play math puzzles and games and then encourage your child to try to invent their own. And, whenever possible, help your child realize a mathematical conclusion with real and tangible results. For example, measure out a full glass of juice with a measuring cup and then ask your child to drink half. Measure what is left. Does it measure half of a cup?

Read books that make math exciting:
- Fractals, Googols and Other Mathematical Tales introduces an animated cat who explains fractals, tangrams and other mathematical concepts you've probably never heard of to children in terms they can understand. This book can double as a great text book by using one story per lesson.
- A Wrinkle in Time is a well-loved classic, combining fantasy and science.
- The Joy of Mathematics helps adults explore the beauty of mathematics that is all around.
- The Math Curse is an amusing book for 4-8 year olds.
- The Gnarly Gnews is a free, humorous bi-monthly newsletter on mathematics.

- The Phantom Tollbooth is an Alice in Wonderland-style adventure into the worlds of words and numbers.
- Use the internet to help your child explore the fascinating world of mathematics.
- Web Math provides a powerful set of math-solvers that gives you instant answers to the stickiest problems.
- Math League has challenging math materials and contests for fourth grade and above.
- Silver Burdett Ginn Mathematics offers Internet-based math activities for grades K-6.
- The Gallery of Interactive Geometry is full of fascinating, interactive geometry activities.

Math is very much like a language of its own. And like any second language, it will get rusty if it is not practiced enough. For that reason, students should always be looking into new ways to keep understanding and brushing up on their math skills, to be certain that foundations do not crumble, inhibiting the learning of new levels of math.

There are many different books, services and websites that have been developed to take the fear out of math, and to help even the most uncertain student develop self confidence in his or her math capabilities.

There is no reason for math or math classes to be a frightening experience, nor should it drive a student crazy, making them believe that they simply don't have the "math brain" that is needed to solve certain problems.

There are friendly ways to tackle such problems and it's all a matter of dispelling myths and creating a solid math foundation.

Concentrate on re-learning the basics and feeling better about yourself in math, and you'll find that the math brain you've always wanted, was there all along.

Special Report: Additional Bonus Material

Due to our efforts to try to keep this book to a manageable length, we've created a link that will give you access to all of your additional bonus material.

Please visit http://www.mcas-test.org/bonuses to access the information.